Power Maths

Year 3
Textbook 3C

Series Editor: Tony Staneff

W0019483

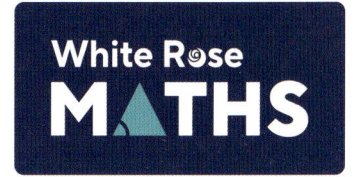

White Rose MATHS

White Rose Maths Edition

Dexter

Dexter is determined.

He likes to help if you get stuck.

helpful

Sparks

flexible

Flo

brave

Astrid

curious

Ash

Series editor: Tony Staneff
Lead author: Josh Lury
Consultants (first edition): Professor Liu Jian and Professor Zhang Dan
Author team (first edition): Tony Staneff, Josh Lury, Tim Handley, Belle Cottingham and Paul Wrangles

P Pearson

Contents

Your teacher will tell you which page you need.

Let's go and find some new maths adventures!

3

How to use this book

These pages make sure we are ready for the unit ahead. Find out what we will be learning and brush up on your skills!

Discover

Lessons start with **Discover**.

Here, we explore new maths problems.

Can you work out how to find the answer?

Do not be afraid to make mistakes. Learn from them and try again!

Share

Next, we share our ideas with the class.

Did we all solve the problems the same way? What ideas can you try?

Think together

Then we have a go at some more problems together. Use what you have just learnt to help you.

We will try a challenge too!

This tells you which page to go to in your **Practice Book**.

At the end of each unit there is an **End of unit check**. This is our chance to show how much we have learnt.

Unit II
Fractions ②

In this unit we will …
- ⚡ Add and subtract fractions
- ⚡ Calculate fractions of a set of objects
- ⚡ Find fractions of amounts
- ⚡ Solve word problems about fractions
- ⚡ Solve word problems about finding fractions of amounts and measures

Do you remember what this is called? Use it to find what fraction is $\frac{3}{8}$ more than $\frac{1}{8}$.

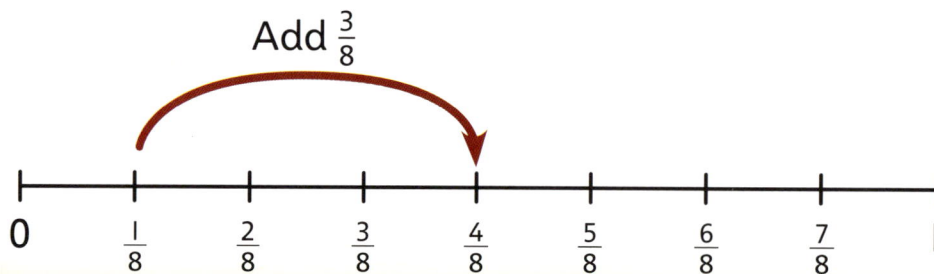

Add $\frac{3}{8}$

0, $\frac{1}{8}$, $\frac{2}{8}$, $\frac{3}{8}$, $\frac{4}{8}$, $\frac{5}{8}$, $\frac{6}{8}$, $\frac{7}{8}$, 1

We will need some maths words.
Which of these have you met before?

numerator   denominator

add   subtract   fraction

whole   equal to   multiply

divide   parts   set of objects

We will need fraction strips too. Use the information in the fraction strip and number line to work out what fraction is shaded.

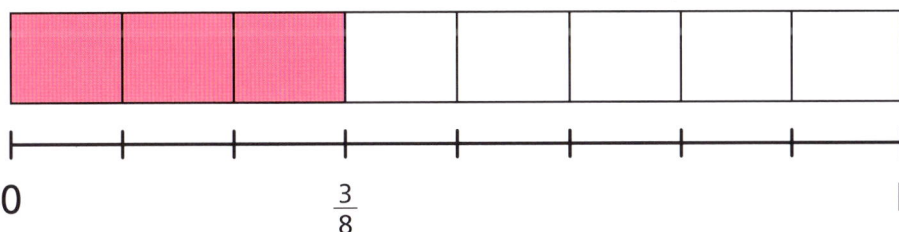

0          $\frac{3}{8}$ 1

Add fractions

Discover

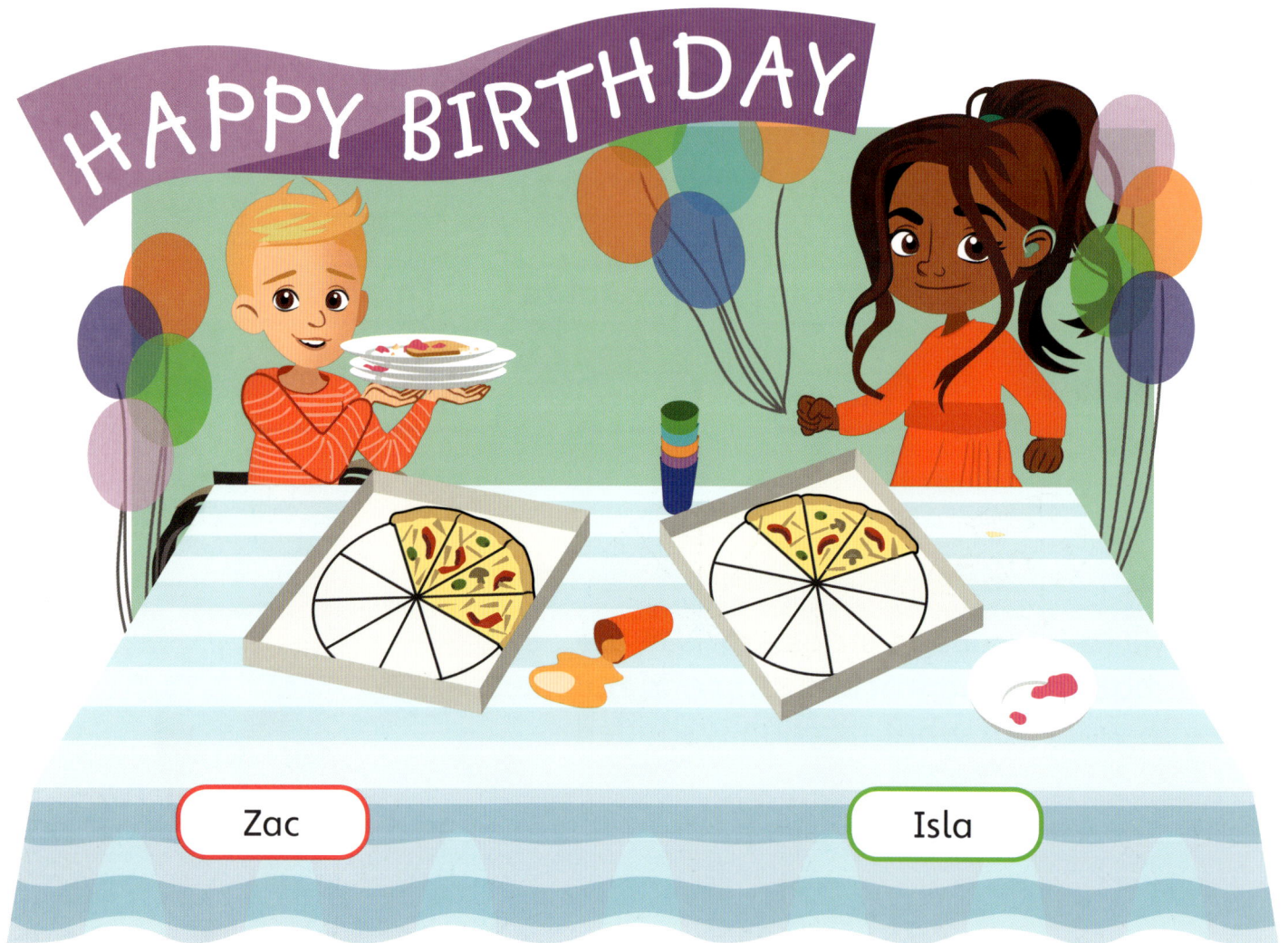

Zac

Isla

1 a) What fraction of the pizza does Zac have left?

What fraction of the pizza does Isla have left?

b) Add these two fractions together.

Share

a) Each pizza is divided into 10 equal parts.

Zac has $\frac{4}{10}$ of the pizza left.

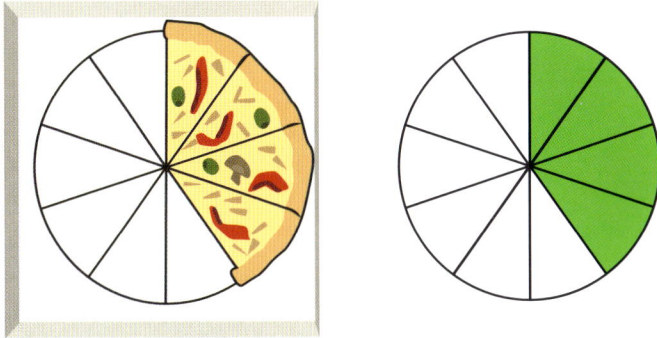

Isla has $\frac{3}{10}$ of the pizza left.

b)

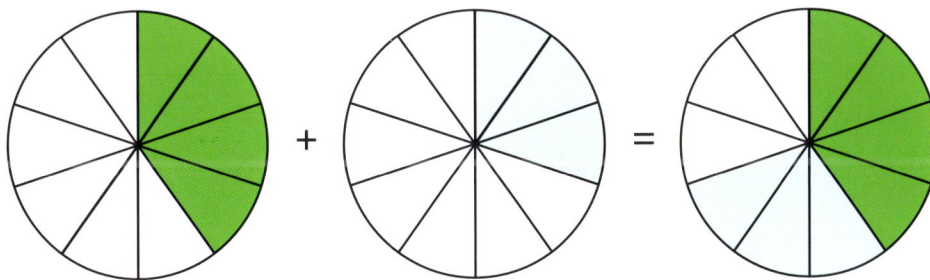

4 tenths + 3 tenths = 7 tenths

$$\frac{4}{10} + \frac{3}{10} = \frac{7}{10}$$

Think together

1 Add these fractions.

a) $\frac{4}{8} + \frac{1}{8} = \dfrac{\boxed{}}{\boxed{}}$

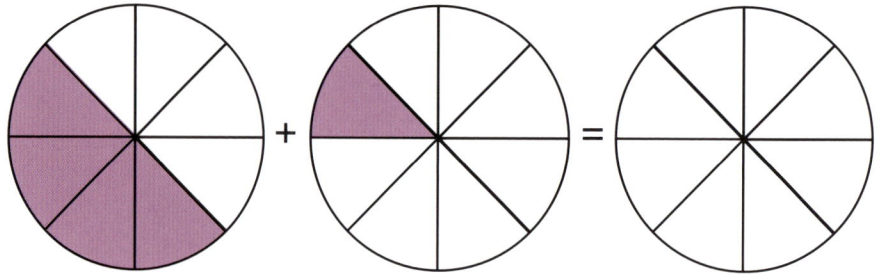

b) $\frac{4}{9} + \frac{2}{9} = \dfrac{\boxed{}}{\boxed{}}$

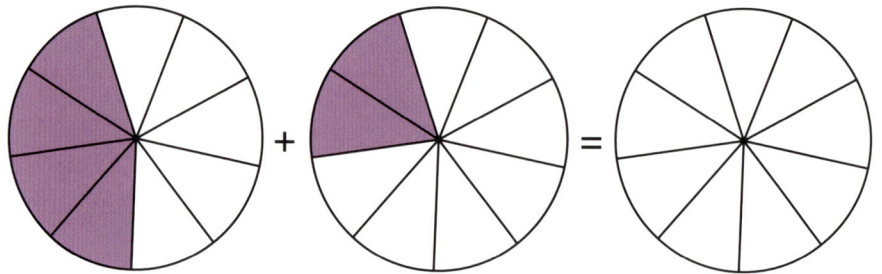

2 a) Use the fraction strip to work out $\frac{2}{5} + \frac{1}{5}$.

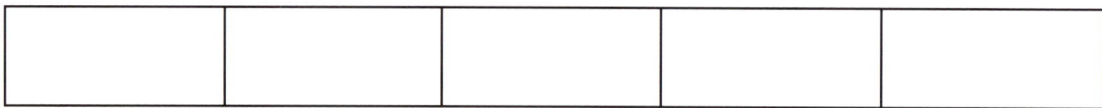

b) What calculation is shown by this fraction strip?

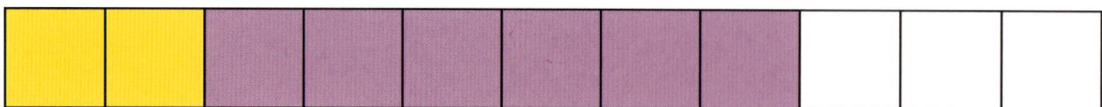

CHALLENGE

3 **a)** Add these fractions.

i) $\dfrac{3}{5} + \dfrac{1}{5} = \dfrac{\square}{\square}$

iii) $\dfrac{1}{6} + \dfrac{3}{6} = \dfrac{\square}{\square}$

ii) $\dfrac{5}{12} + \dfrac{1}{12} = \dfrac{\square}{\square}$

iv) $\dfrac{3}{5} + \dfrac{2}{5} = \dfrac{\square}{\square}$

I will use fraction strips to help me work out the answers.

I don't think I need to use fraction strips. I can see a quicker way of adding the fractions.

b) $\dfrac{\square}{11} + \dfrac{\square}{11} = \dfrac{8}{11}$

How many different answers can you find?

→ Practice book 3C p6

Subtract fractions

Discover

1 a) What fraction of the tank is full of fuel?

Represent this on a fraction strip.

b) How much fuel will be left after the journey home?

Share

a) The dial is divided into 8 equal sections.

The tank is $\frac{5}{8}$ full.

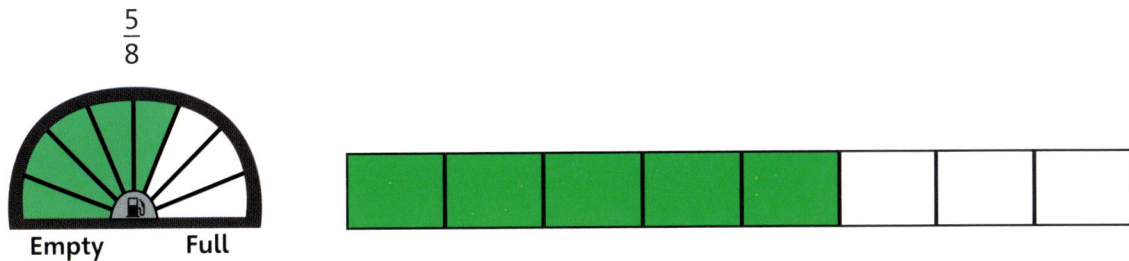

$\frac{5}{8}$

b) The journey home will use $\frac{3}{8}$ of a tank of fuel.

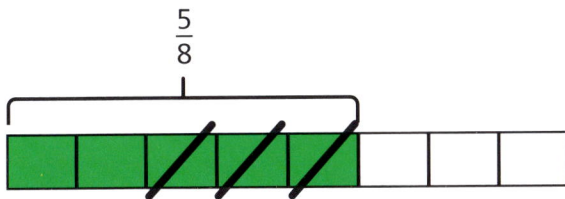

$\frac{5}{8}$

> I drew a fraction strip and shaded in $\frac{5}{8}$.
> Then I crossed out $\frac{3}{8}$.

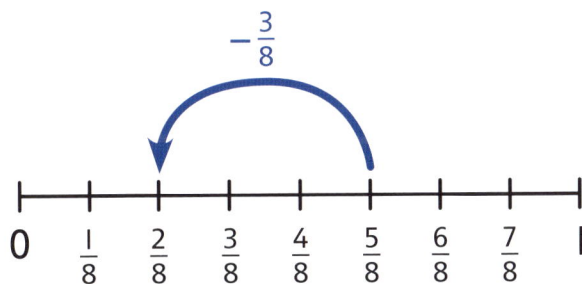

$-\frac{3}{8}$

> I started at $\frac{5}{8}$ on a number line and I jumped back $\frac{3}{8}$.

$$0 \quad \frac{1}{8} \quad \frac{2}{8} \quad \frac{3}{8} \quad \frac{4}{8} \quad \frac{5}{8} \quad \frac{6}{8} \quad \frac{7}{8} \quad 1$$

5 eighths − 3 eighths = 2 eighths

$$\frac{5}{8} - \frac{3}{8} = \frac{2}{8}$$

There will be $\frac{2}{8}$ of a tank of fuel left after the journey home.

Think together

1 Complete these subtractions.

a) $\dfrac{7}{8} - \dfrac{5}{8} = \dfrac{\square}{\square}$

b) $\dfrac{9}{10} - \dfrac{2}{10} = \dfrac{\square}{10}$

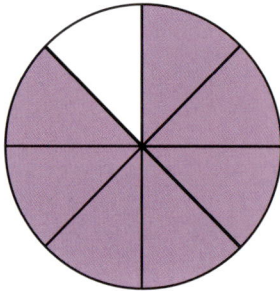

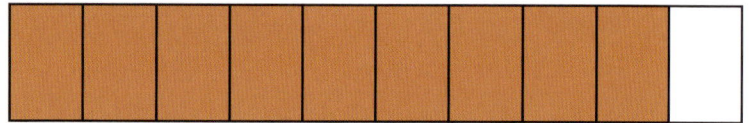

2 Work out

a) $\dfrac{4}{5} - \dfrac{1}{5}$

b) $\dfrac{5}{7} - \dfrac{1}{7}$

c) $\dfrac{10}{11} - \dfrac{6}{11}$

d) $\dfrac{7}{8} - \dfrac{7}{8}$

I will cross out the right number of parts.

CHALLENGE

3 **a)** Complete the calculation.

$$\frac{\square}{7} - \frac{\square}{7} = \frac{2}{7}$$

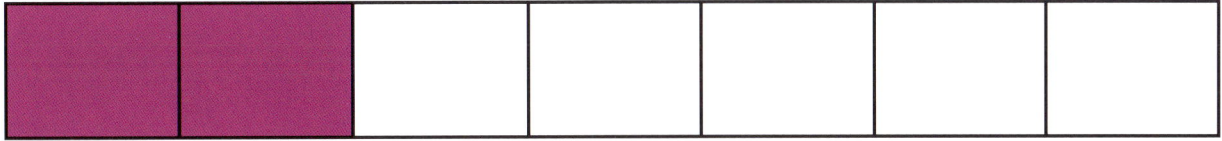

I think I can find more than one answer.

b) The difference between two fractions is $\frac{3}{10}$.

What could the fractions be?
Use the number line to help you.

I wonder what 'the difference' means.

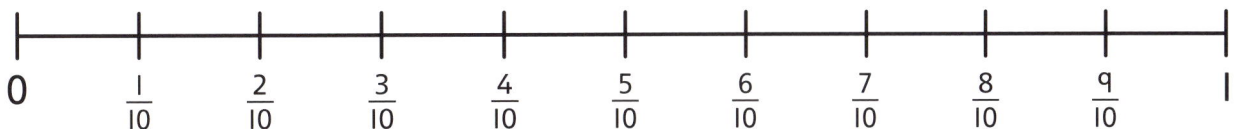

$$0 \quad \frac{1}{10} \quad \frac{2}{10} \quad \frac{3}{10} \quad \frac{4}{10} \quad \frac{5}{10} \quad \frac{6}{10} \quad \frac{7}{10} \quad \frac{8}{10} \quad \frac{9}{10} \quad 1$$

→ **Practice book 3C p9**

Partition the whole

Discover

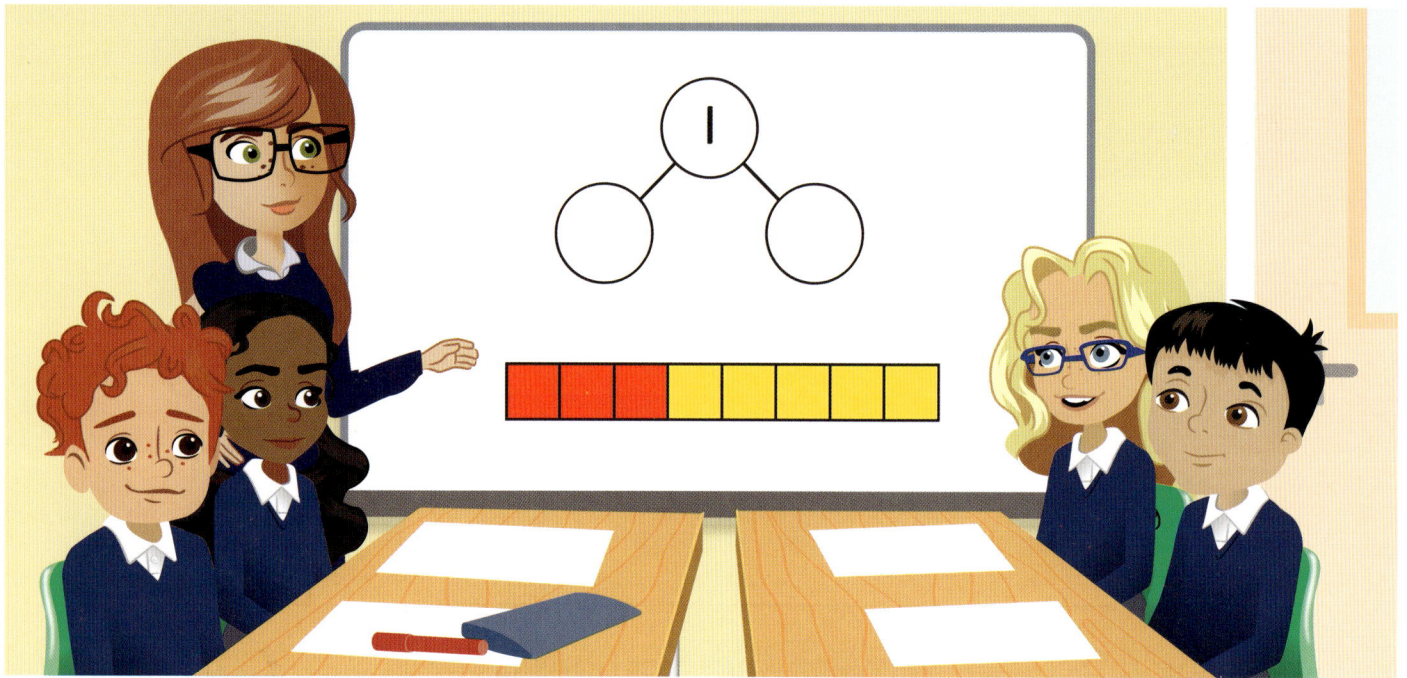

1 **a)** Complete the part-whole model for the fraction strip.

   b) Draw another fraction strip with 8 equal parts.

   Shade it in differently.

   Draw a part-whole model for your shading.

Share

a) 3 parts are red and 5 parts are yellow.

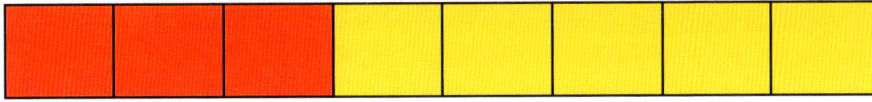

$\frac{3}{8}$ of the strip is red and $\frac{5}{8}$ of the strip is yellow.

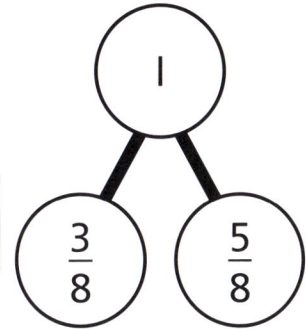

b)

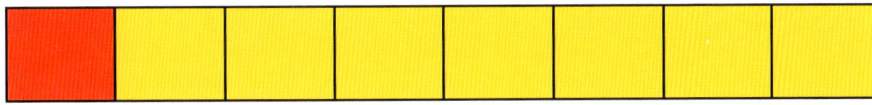

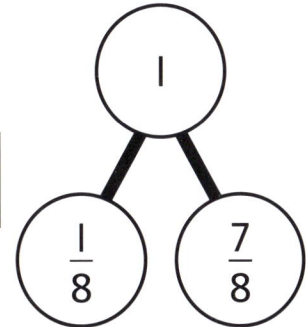

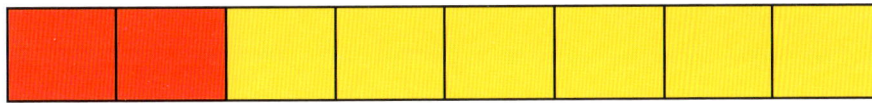

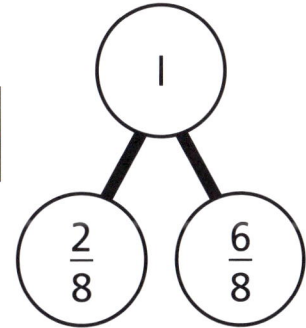

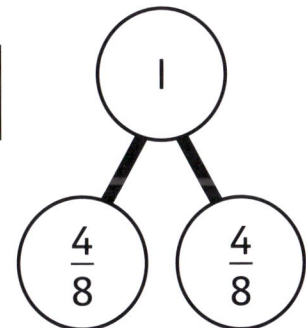

I found all the ways to shade a fraction strip with 8 equal parts.

Think together

1 Complete the part-whole model for the fraction circle.

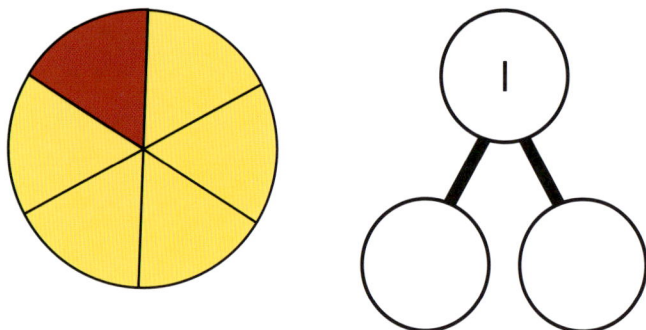

2 Complete the part-whole models.

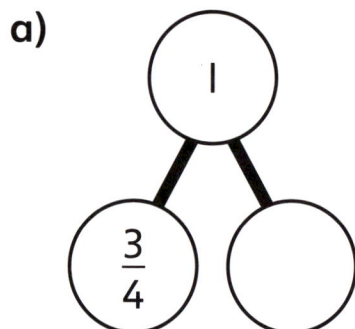

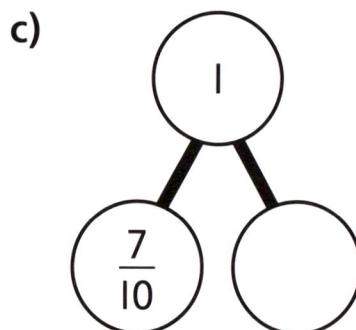

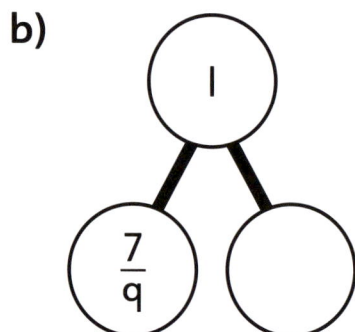

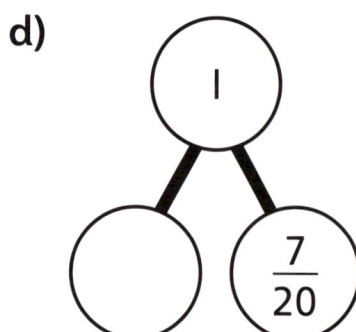

a)

$\frac{3}{4}$

c)

$\frac{7}{10}$

b)

$\frac{7}{9}$

d)

$\frac{7}{20}$

I notice something about the numerators when you add them together.

CHALLENGE

3 **a)** Emma is working out this subtraction.

$$1 - \frac{3}{5}$$

She wants to use this part-whole model and fraction circle to help her.

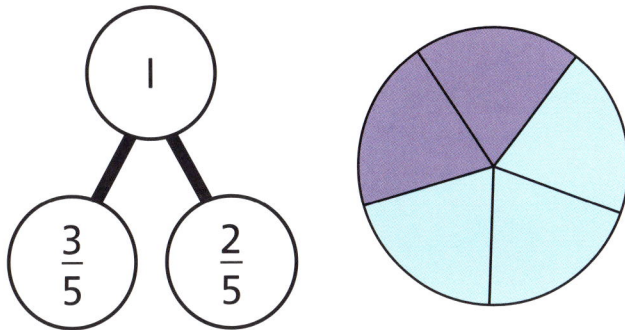

1

$\frac{3}{5}$ $\frac{2}{5}$

How can Emma use the part-whole model to help her?

b) Work out:

$$1 - \frac{2}{3}$$ $$1 - \frac{5}{9}$$ $$1 - \frac{1}{12}$$

I know a way to write a whole as a fraction.

→ Practice book 3C p12

Problem solving – add and subtract fractions

Discover

We used $\frac{1}{10}$ of the food on Monday and $\frac{3}{10}$ of the food on Tuesday.

Sofia

Amal

1 **a)** What fraction of the food did they eat, in total, on Monday and Tuesday?

b) What fraction of the food is left in the box?

Share

a)

I drew a fraction strip to show what fraction of the food they ate on Monday and what fraction they ate on Tuesday.

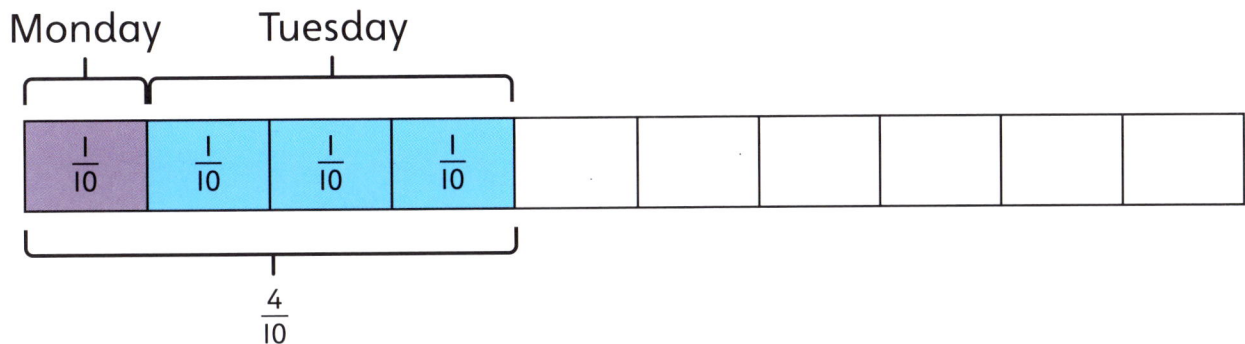

Monday   Tuesday

| $\frac{1}{10}$ | $\frac{1}{10}$ | $\frac{1}{10}$ | $\frac{1}{10}$ | | | | | | |

$\frac{4}{10}$

$\frac{1}{10} + \frac{3}{10} = \frac{4}{10}$, so they ate $\frac{4}{10}$ of the food in total on Monday and Tuesday.

b)

Amount left

| $\frac{1}{10}$ | $\frac{1}{10}$ | $\frac{1}{10}$ | $\frac{1}{10}$ | $\frac{1}{10}$ | $\frac{1}{10}$ | $\frac{1}{10}$ | $\frac{1}{10}$ | $\frac{1}{10}$ | $\frac{1}{10}$ |

$\frac{4}{10}$ $\frac{6}{10}$

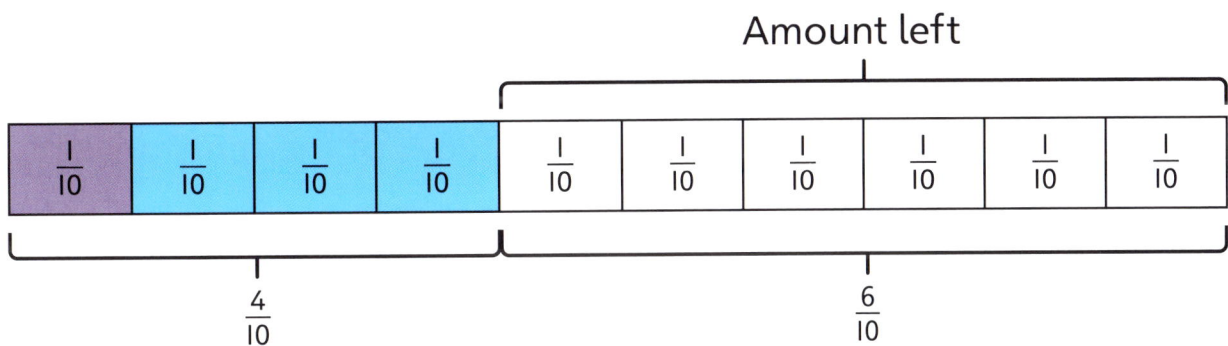

$1 - \frac{4}{10} = \frac{6}{10}$, so $\frac{6}{10}$ of the food is left in the box.

Think together

1 Sofia and Amal go on a journey.

They walk $\frac{5}{8}$ of the journey and ski $\frac{1}{8}$ of the journey.

Then they stop for a rest.

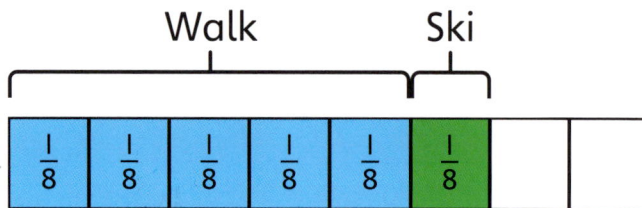

Walk   Ski

| $\frac{1}{8}$ | $\frac{1}{8}$ | $\frac{1}{8}$ | $\frac{1}{8}$ | $\frac{1}{8}$ | $\frac{1}{8}$ | | |

a) What fraction of the journey have they travelled so far?

b) What fraction of the journey is left?

Show your workings clearly. It is important to show every step even if you can see the answer straight away!

2 $\frac{3}{9}$ of the tents at the polar camp are blue, $\frac{1}{9}$ of the tents are red.

The rest of the tents are yellow.

What fraction of the tents are yellow?

I think I can work this out in my head without using a fraction strip.

3 Alex ate $\frac{1}{5}$ of a packet of raisins. Max ate $\frac{1}{5}$ of the packet more than Alex.

CHALLENGE

a) What fraction of the packet of raisins did Alex and Max eat altogether?

First, I will work out what fraction of the packet Max ate.

I will use the fraction strip to represent the fraction that both the children ate.

b) What fraction of the packet is left?

23

→ Practice book 3C p15

Unit fractions of a set of objects

Discover

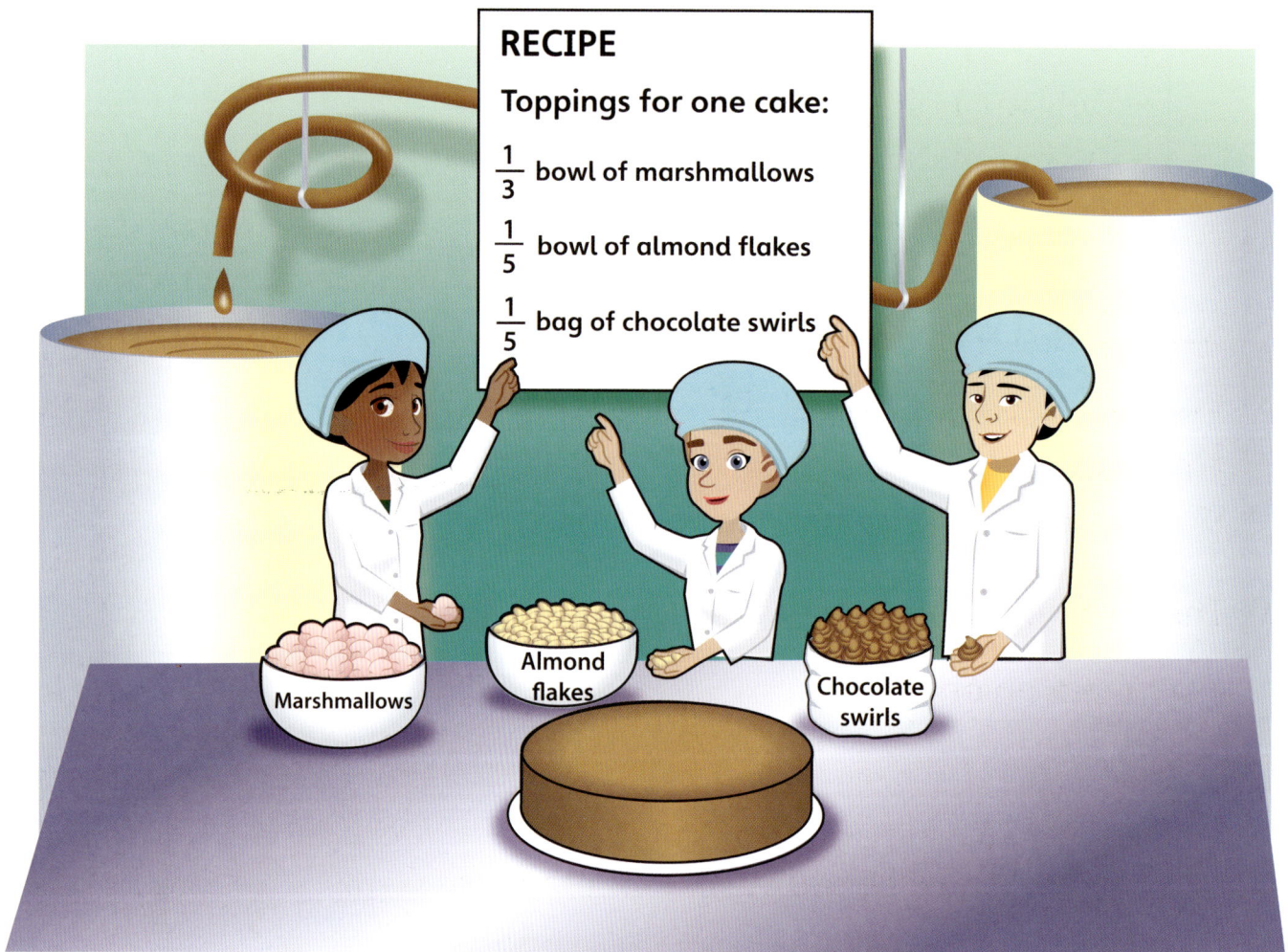

1 **a)** There are 30 marshmallows in a bowl.

How many marshmallows are used on 1 cake?

b) There are 45 chocolate swirls in a bag.

How many chocolate swirls are used on 1 cake?

Share

a) There are 30 marshmallows.

$\frac{1}{3}$ of the marshmallows are used on each cake.

> To find $\frac{1}{3}$ I divided the whole into 3.
> I drew a bar model to help me find $\frac{1}{3}$.

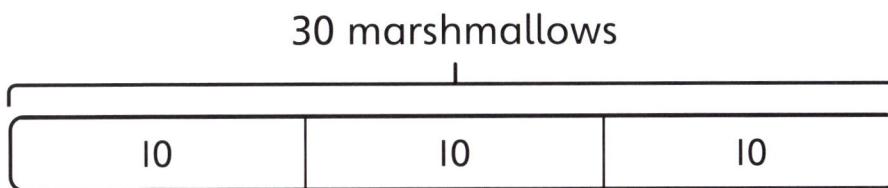

30 marshmallows

10	10	10

$30 \div 3 = 10$
10 marshmallows are needed for 1 cake.

b) There are 45 chocolate swirls.

$\frac{1}{5}$ are used on each cake.

> To find $\frac{1}{5}$ I divided the whole into 5.
> I divided by 5 as this is the denominator.

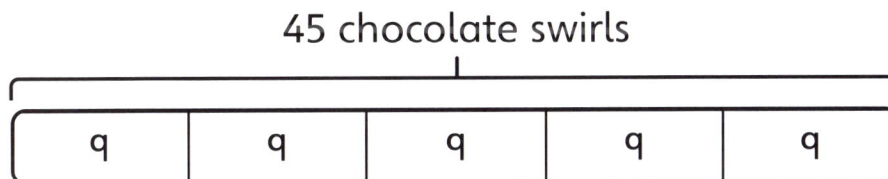

45 chocolate swirls

9	9	9	9	9

$45 \div 5 = 9$
9 chocolate swirls are needed for 1 cake.

Think together

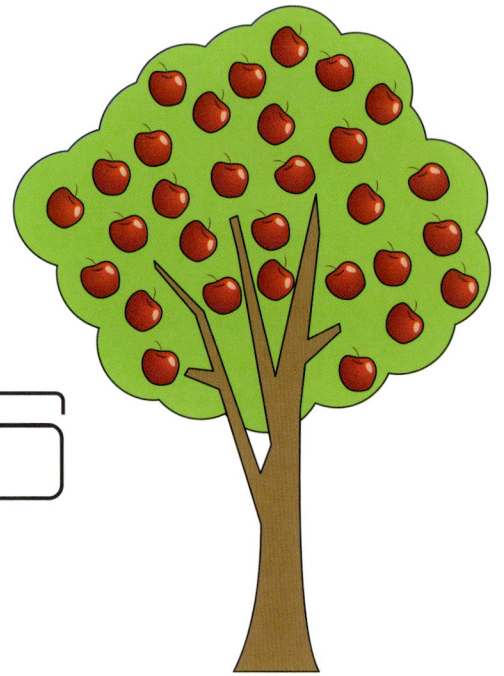

1 Find $\frac{1}{6}$ of 30 apples.

?					

2 Max, Emma and Ebo have 18 footballs.

They share the footballs equally between themselves.

(Max) (Emma) (Ebo)

How many balls will they get each?

3 **a)** Work out:

$\dfrac{1}{2}$ of £24

$\dfrac{1}{3}$ of £24

$\dfrac{1}{4}$ of £24

$\dfrac{1}{12}$ of £24

Discuss with a partner how you answered these questions.

b) $\dfrac{1}{\boxed{}}$ of 24 = 3

What is the denominator?

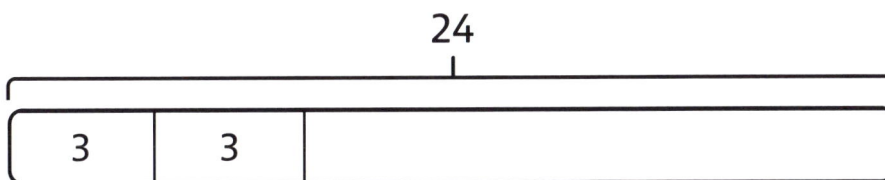

24

| 3 | 3 | |

I will draw a bar model for each one and divide the whole into a different number of parts.

So when I divide 24 into an equal number of parts, each part is worth 3. I now need to work out how many equal parts there are.

27

→ Practice book 3C p18

Non-unit fractions of a set of objects

Discover

RECIPE

Toppings for one cake:

$\frac{2}{3}$ bowl of chocolate chips

$\frac{2}{5}$ bowl of raspberries

$\frac{3}{7}$ bag of strawberry laces

Chocolate chips

Raspberries

Strawberry laces

1 **a)** Find $\frac{1}{5}$ of 35.

Draw a diagram to explain your answer.

b) There are 35 raspberries in a bowl.

How many raspberries are needed for 1 cake?

Share

a)

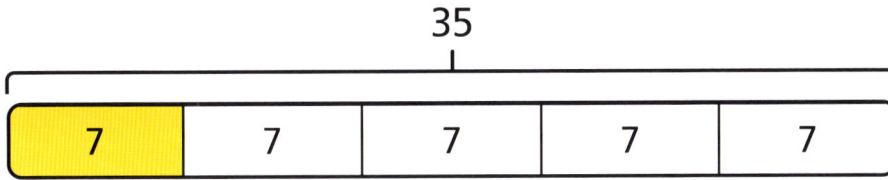

$35 \div 5 = 7$

$\frac{1}{5}$ of $35 = 7$

b) There are 35 raspberries in a bowl.

$\frac{2}{5}$ are used on 1 cake.

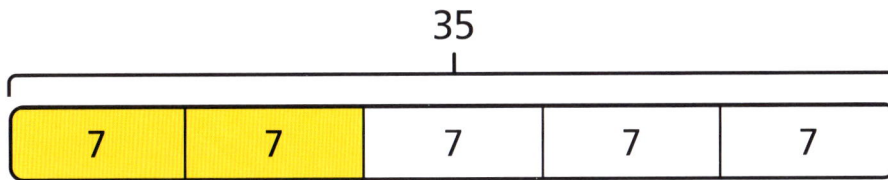

$\frac{1}{5}$ of $35 = 7$

$7 \times 2 = 14$

$\frac{2}{5}$ of $35 = 14$

14 raspberries are needed for 1 cake.

I knew that each part of the bar model is $\frac{1}{5}$. So to find $\frac{2}{5}$, I multiplied by 2.

Think together

1 Aki has 18 cherries.

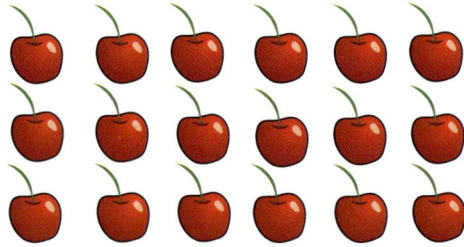

a) Find $\frac{1}{6}$ of 18 cherries.

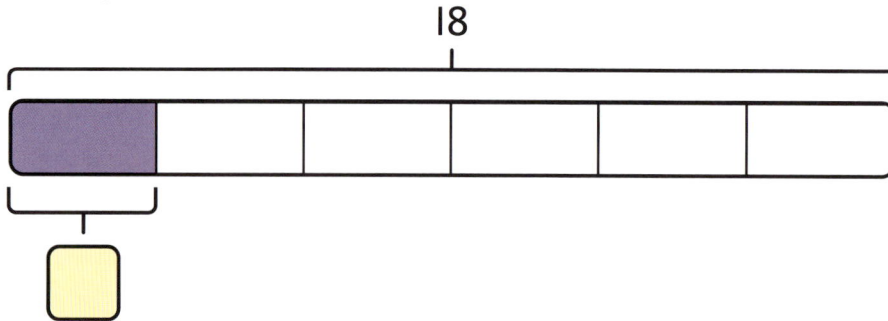

18

b) Find $\frac{4}{6}$ of 18 cherries.

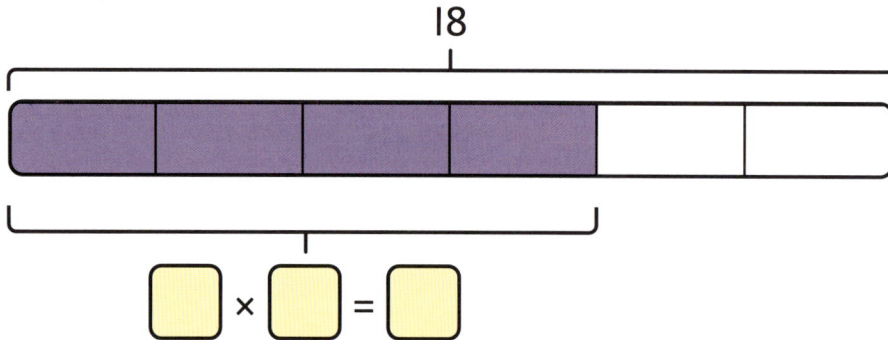

18

$\boxed{} \times \boxed{} = \boxed{}$

c) Find $\frac{5}{6}$ of 18 cherries.

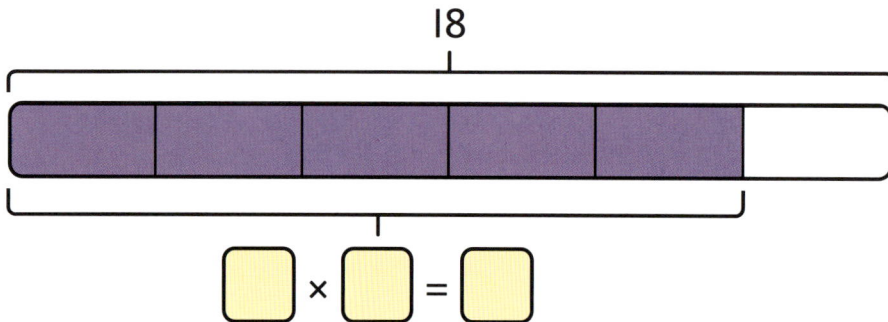

18

$\boxed{} \times \boxed{} = \boxed{}$

30

2 **a)** Work out $\frac{2}{3}$ of 12 apples.

b) Work out $\frac{3}{10}$ of 40.

I will draw a bar model to show each one.

CHALLENGE

3 Andy has won a competition.

He can choose from two prizes.

A

Prize!
$\frac{3}{5}$ of 15 coins

B

Prize!
$\frac{3}{4}$ of 12 coins

Show that both prizes give the same number of coins.

I wonder if I can use the arrays of coins to check my answer or to help me explain.

31

Reason with fractions of an amount

Discover

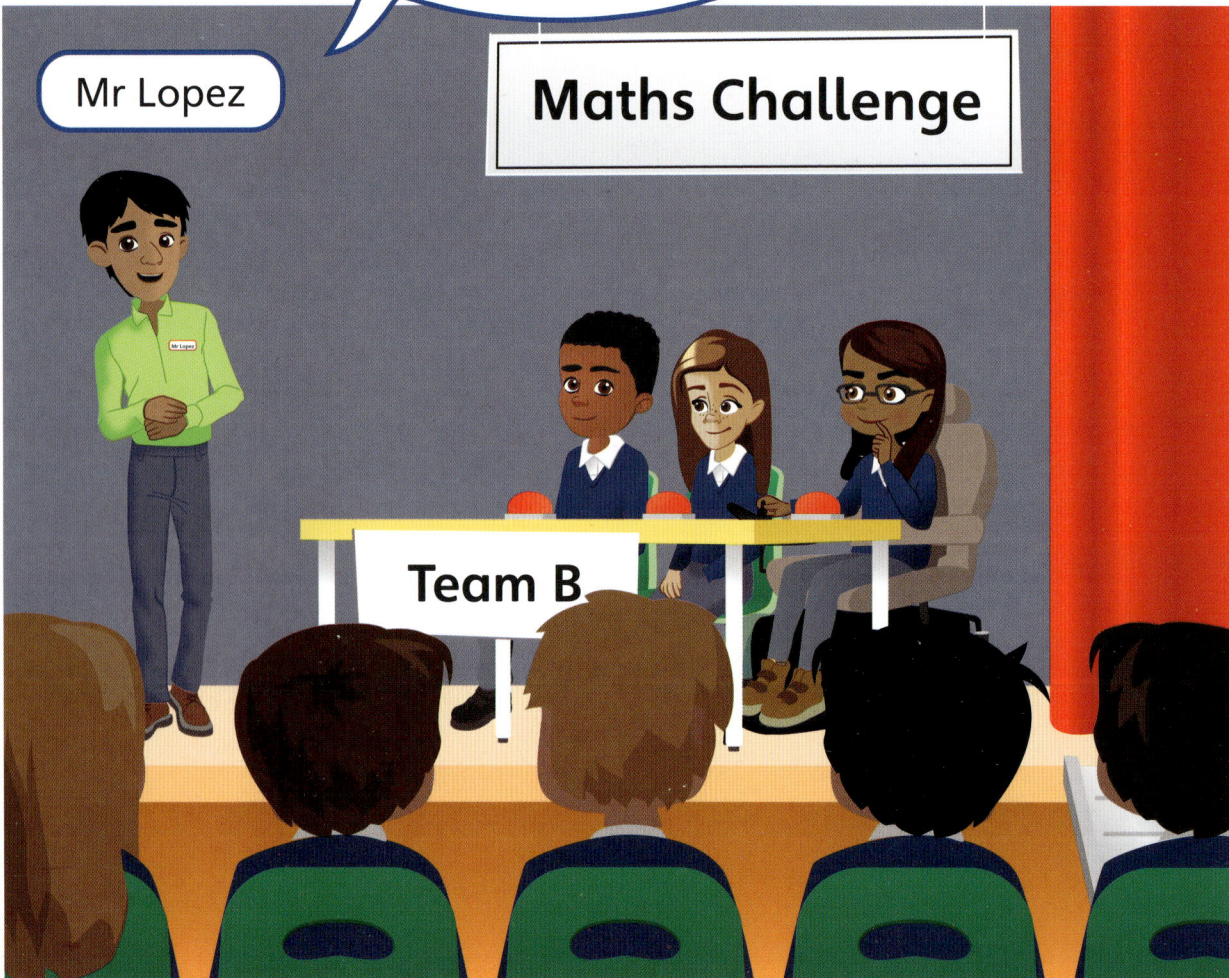

Mr Lopez: $\frac{1}{10}$ of my number is 6. What is my number?

1 **a)** Work out Mr Lopez's number.

b) What is $\frac{9}{10}$ of Mr Lopez's number?

Share

a) $\frac{1}{10}$ of Mr Lopez's number is equal to 6.

Mr Lopez's number

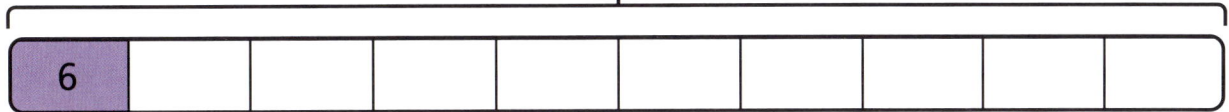

6									

To work out the number, multiply 10 × 6.
Mr Lopez's number is 60.

b)

> I multiplied $\frac{1}{10}$ of the number by 9 to find $\frac{9}{10}$.

9 × 6 = 54

6	6	6	6	6	6	6	6	6	

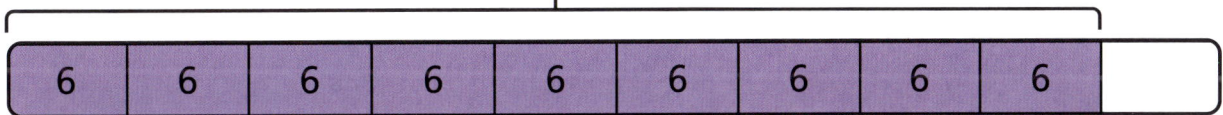

> I did it a different way. I knew that the whole is 60 and I subtracted $\frac{1}{10}$.

60 − 6 = 54

6	6	6	6	6	6	6	6	6	6

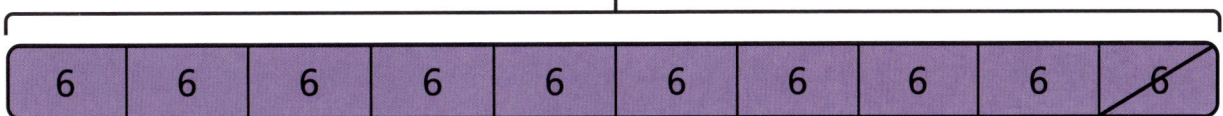

$\frac{9}{10}$ of Mr Lopez's number is 54.

Think together

1

$\frac{1}{8}$ of my number is equal to 3.

Reena

3							

What is Reena's number?

2

$\frac{2}{5}$ of my number is equal to 12.

Richard

12

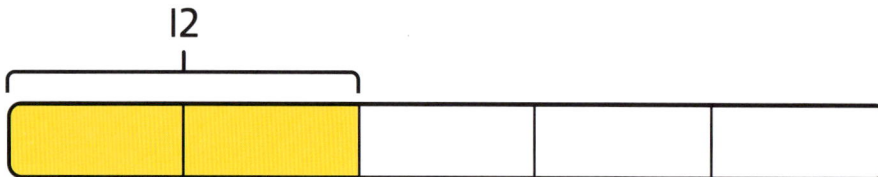

a) What is $\frac{1}{5}$ of Richard's number?

b) What is Richard's number?

c) What is $\frac{4}{5}$ of Richard's number?

d) What is $\frac{9}{10}$ of Richard's number?

3

CHALLENGE

I can find $\frac{1}{6}$ of the total of Reena's and Richard's numbers quickly.

Danny

Discuss two ways Danny could find $\frac{1}{6}$ of the total of Richard's and Reena's number.

I think Danny could find $\frac{1}{6}$ of each number and add the numbers together.

I wonder if I could do something with the numbers first and still get the same answer.

35

→ **Practice book 3C p24**

Problem solving – fractions of measures

Discover

I have 20 kg of fish in my bucket.

1 **a)** The zookeeper feeds the penguins $\frac{2}{5}$ of the bucket of fish.

How many kilograms of fish do the penguins get?

b) How many kilograms of fish are left in the bucket?

Share

a) There are 20 kg of fish in the bucket.

$\frac{2}{5}$ of the fish are fed to the penguins.

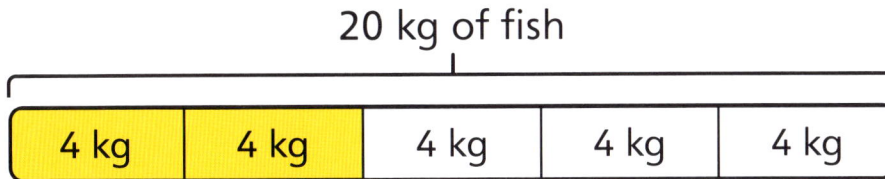

20 kg of fish

4 kg	4 kg	4 kg	4 kg	4 kg

20 kg ÷ 5 = 4 kg

2 × 4 kg = 8 kg

The zookeeper feeds the penguins 8 kg of fish.

b) There were 20 kg of fish in the bucket.

8 kg of the fish were fed to the penguins.

20 kg – 8 kg = 12 kg

There are 12 kg of fish left.

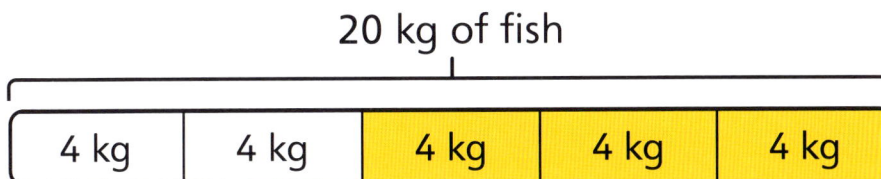

> I subtracted to work out how many kg of fish were left.

Or:

$\frac{2}{5}$ of the fish were fed to the penguins, therefore $\frac{3}{5}$ of the fish were left.

3 × 4 kg = 12 kg

20 kg of fish

4 kg	4 kg	4 kg	4 kg	4 kg

Think together

1 There are 24 frogs.

$\frac{1}{8}$ of the frogs are orange.

$\frac{5}{8}$ of the frogs are green.

The rest of the frogs are yellow.

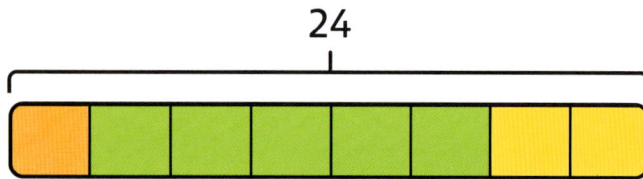

24

a) How many orange and green frogs are there altogether?

b) How many yellow frogs are there?

I can see two ways to work out the number of yellow frogs.

2 Max has a box of 48 treats.

He gives $\frac{5}{6}$ of the treats to some animals.

How many treats does he have left?

CHALLENGE

3 In the zoo feed store there is:

$\frac{1}{4}$ of a 800 g bag of feed.

$\frac{3}{4}$ of a 200 g bag of feed.

The zebras need 450 g of feed.

Is there enough feed?

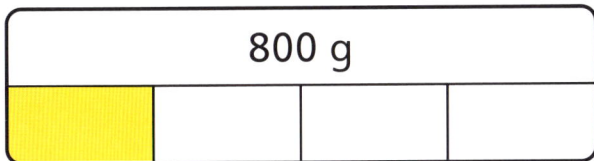

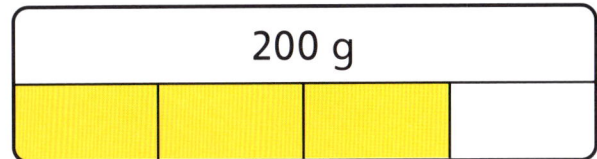

800 g

200 g

800 g

200 g

I wonder how I can divide 800 by 4. I will think of 800 as 8 hundreds to help me with the division.

I will halve and then halve again.

→ Practice book 3C p27

End of unit check

1 Work out $\frac{2}{7} + \frac{3}{7}$

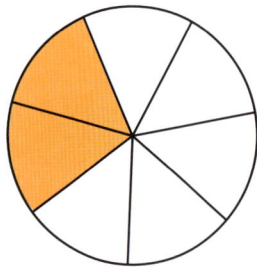

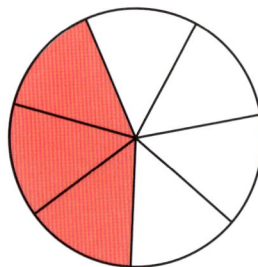

A $\frac{5}{14}$ **B** $\frac{5}{7}$ **C** 5   **D** $\frac{6}{7}$

2 What is the missing part?

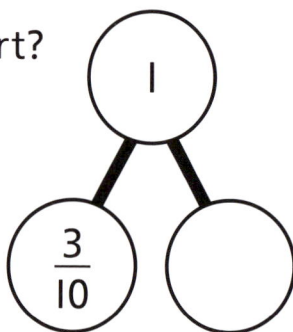

1

$\frac{3}{10}$

A $\frac{3}{7}$ **B** 7   **C** $\frac{7}{10}$ **D** $\frac{2}{10}$

3 What is $\frac{2}{3}$ of 18 kg?

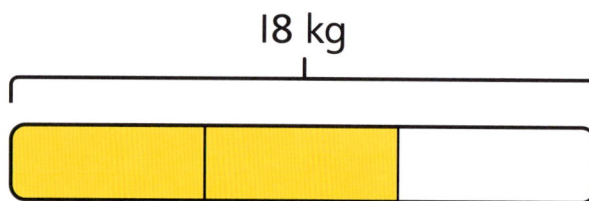

18 kg

A 36 kg   **B** 18 kg   **C** 12 kg   **D** 6 kg

4 Which fraction cannot go into any of these fraction sentences?

$\frac{3}{5} + \frac{\square}{\square} = 1$ $\frac{7}{10} + \frac{\square}{\square} = 1$ $\frac{\square}{\square} + \frac{1}{8} = 1$

A $\frac{3}{5}$ **B** $\frac{7}{8}$ **C** $\frac{2}{5}$ **D** $\frac{3}{10}$

5 Jake painted $\frac{1}{6}$ of the wall on Monday and $\frac{3}{6}$ of the wall on Tuesday.

What fraction of the wall was not painted?

```
├────────┼────────┼────────┼────────┼────────┼────────┤
0                                                        1
```

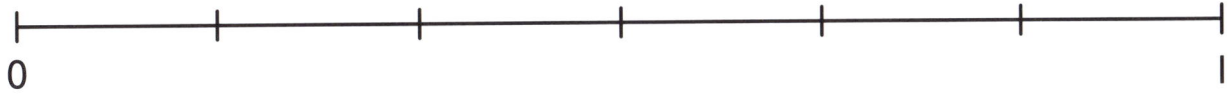

A $\frac{2}{6}$ B $\frac{4}{6}$ C $\frac{2}{3}$ D $\frac{1}{2}$

6 Which numbers could be the missing numerator?

$\frac{5}{8}$ of 40 kg $< \dfrac{\square}{5}$ of 40 kg

A 1 and 2   C 3 and 4

B 2 and 3   D 4 and 5

40 kg

$\frac{1}{8}$	$\frac{1}{8}$	$\frac{1}{8}$	$\frac{1}{8}$	$\frac{1}{8}$	$\frac{1}{8}$	$\frac{1}{8}$	$\frac{1}{8}$

$\frac{1}{5}$	$\frac{1}{5}$	$\frac{1}{5}$	$\frac{1}{5}$	$\frac{1}{5}$

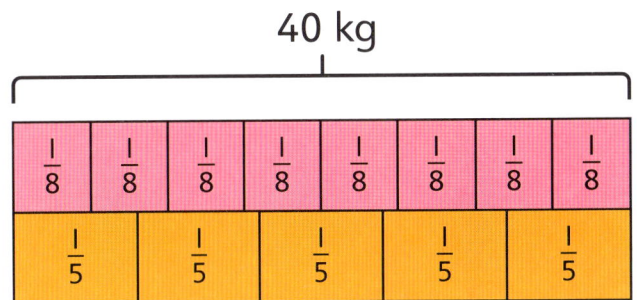

7 Complete the addition pyramid.

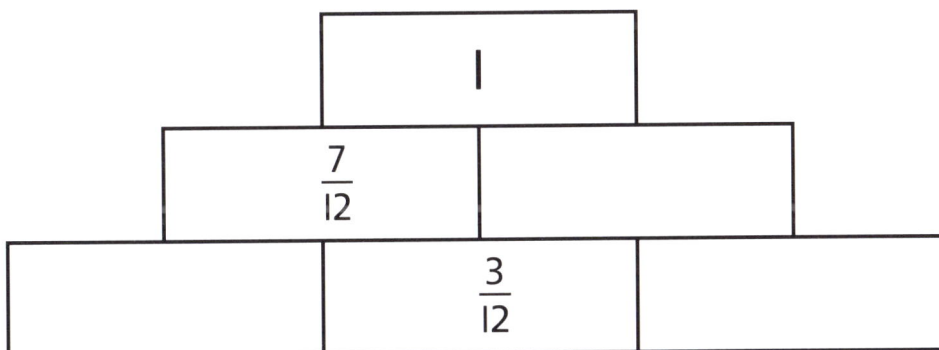

```
              ┌───────────┐
              │     1     │
          ┌───┴───┬───────┴───┐
          │  7    │           │
          │ ──    │           │
          │ 12    │           │
      ┌───┴───┬───┴───┬───────┴───┐
      │       │  3    │           │
      │       │ ──    │           │
      │       │ 12    │           │
      └───────┴───────┴───────────┘
```

➜ Practice book 3C p30

Unit 12
Money

In this unit we will …

⚡ Record money in £ and p

⚡ Convert money

⚡ Add and subtract amounts of money

⚡ Solve problems including ones that involve finding change

In Year 2, we counted money in pounds and in pence. How much money is here?

We will need some maths words.
How many of these can you remember?

pounds (£)   pence (p)

convert   total

difference   change

We will also need to be able to add and subtract numbers. What calculations are shown here?

H	T	O
	5	6
+	7	9
1	3	5
	1	

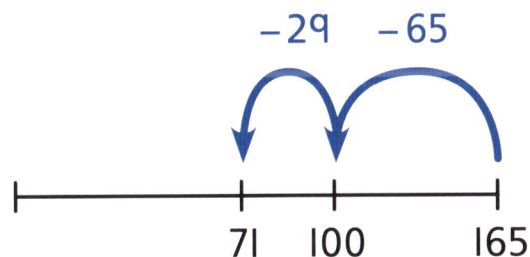

−29   −65

71   100   165

Pounds and pence

Discover

Sofia

Lee

1 **a)** How much money does Lee have?

b) Sofia has these coins in her purse:

She gives Lee £2 and 28p.

Which coins did Sofia give Lee?

Key 1p 2p 5p 10p 20p 50p £1 £2

Share

a) Sort the notes and coins into pounds (£) and pence (p).

> I counted the pounds first and then the pence.
> I used a number line to find the total amount.
> I started with the highest value.

£5   £7   £9   £11   £12

Lee has 12 pounds.

50p   70p   80p   82p   84p   86p   87p   88p

Lee has 88 pence.

Lee has £12 and 88p.

b) Sofia gave Lee a £2 coin and 20p, 5p, 2p and 1p coins.

£2

20p   25p   27p   28p

£5   £10   £20   £50

Think together

1 How much money does Sofia have?

Sofia has ⬜ pounds and ⬜ pence.

Sofia has £ ⬜ and ⬜ p.

2 Lee takes 25 pounds and 37 pence from his money box.

Choose some of the notes and coins to make this amount.

Key 1p 2p 5p 10p 20p 50p £1 £2

3 Sofia is trying to make £1 with different numbers of coins.
Complete the table using one more coin in each row.

CHALLENGE

I have £1 in total. I have fewer than 10 coins.

I remember that 100 pence is equal to £1.

Number of coins	Possible
1	
2	
3	Not possible
4	
5	
6	
7	
8	
9	

Convert pounds and pence

Discover

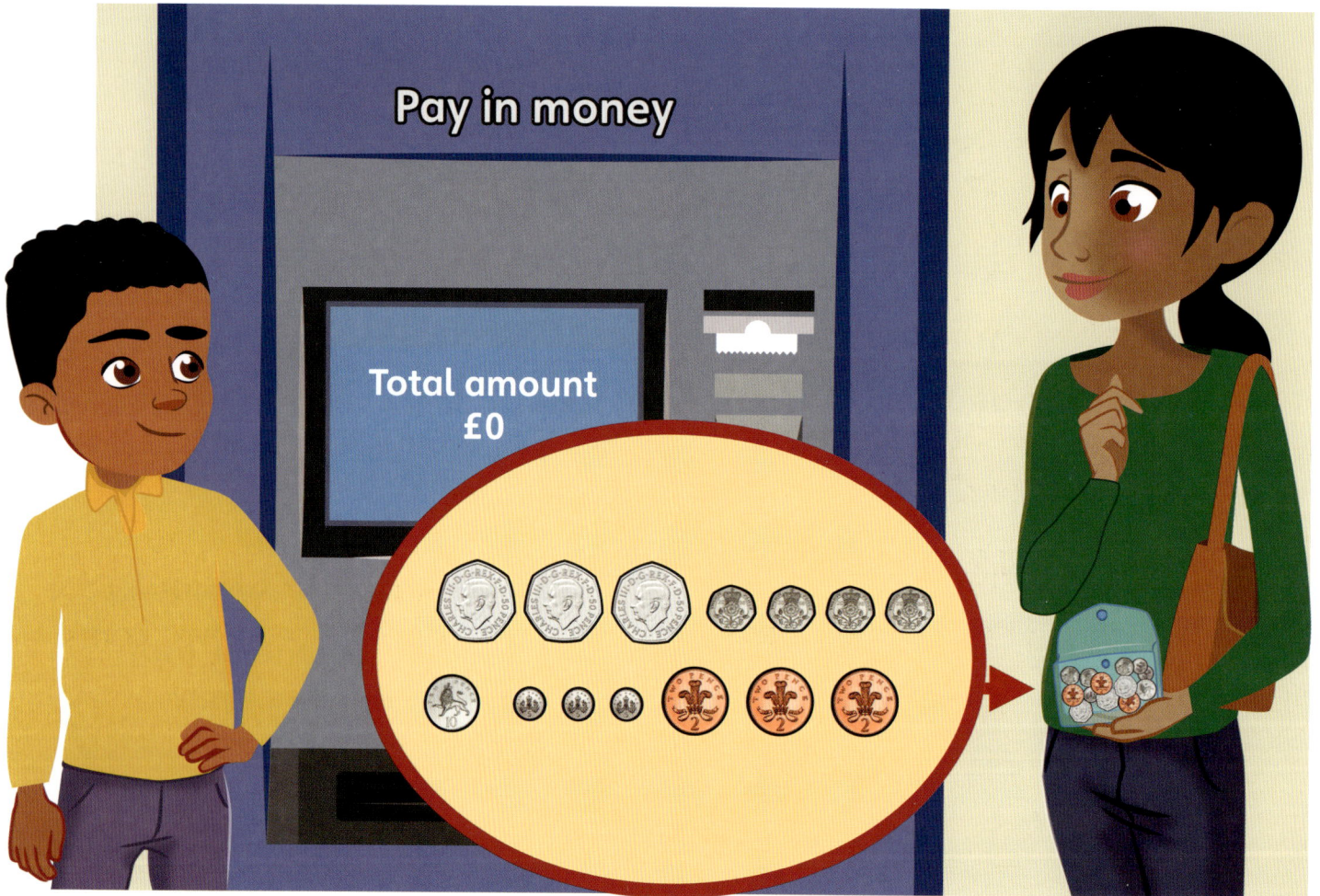

Pay in money

Total amount
£0

Lee

Sofia

1 a) How much money does Sofia put into the machine?

b) Lee puts in £1 using some silver coins. They are all the same coin.

What could he have put in?

Key 1p 2p 5p 10p 20p 50p £1 £2

Share

a) There are 100 pence in a pound.

> I put together coins that make £1 first. Then I counted the coins left over. There are different ways to make £1.

100p = £1

100p = £1

61p

261p = £2 and 61p

Sofia puts £2 and 61p into the machine.

> I worked out how many coins made £1 for each of the silver coins.

b) Lee could have put in these coins:

Two 50p coins

Ten 10p coins

Five 20p coins

Twenty 5p coins

£5   £10   £20   £50

Think together

1 **a)** Which of these sets of coins make £1?

b) How much money does Holly have?

2 Complete the part-whole models.

a)

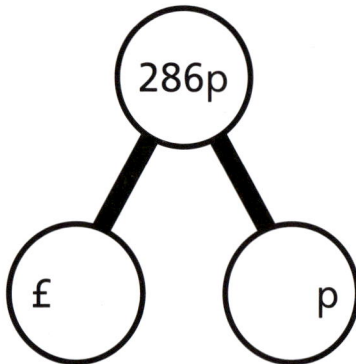

b)

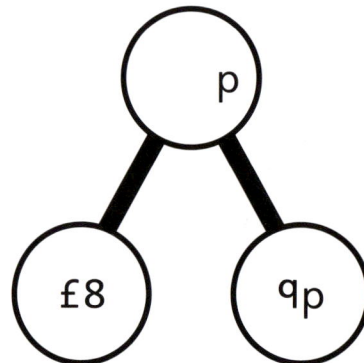

Key 1p 2p 5p 10p 20p 50p £1 £2

3 Mr Jones has some bags of coins.

Convert between pounds and pence.

CHALLENGE

a)

□p

£1 and 52p

c)

□p

£4 and 75p

b)

568p

£□ and □p

d)

307p

£□ and □p

Draw, or use coins, to show what coins could be in each bag.

> I am going to make the pounds first, and then the pence.

> I know that £1 is equal to 100p. I will convert everything to pence first.

£5   £10   £20   £50

→ Practice book 3C p35

Unit 12: Money, Lesson 3

Add money

Discover

Can I have a cup of tea and a slice of cake, please?

Tea – £1 and 20p

Small coffee – £1 and 80p

Large coffee – £2 and 20p

Juice – £1 and 45p

Water – 79p

Toastie – £2 and 80p

Slice of cake – £2 and 32p

Strawberry tart – £3 and 58p

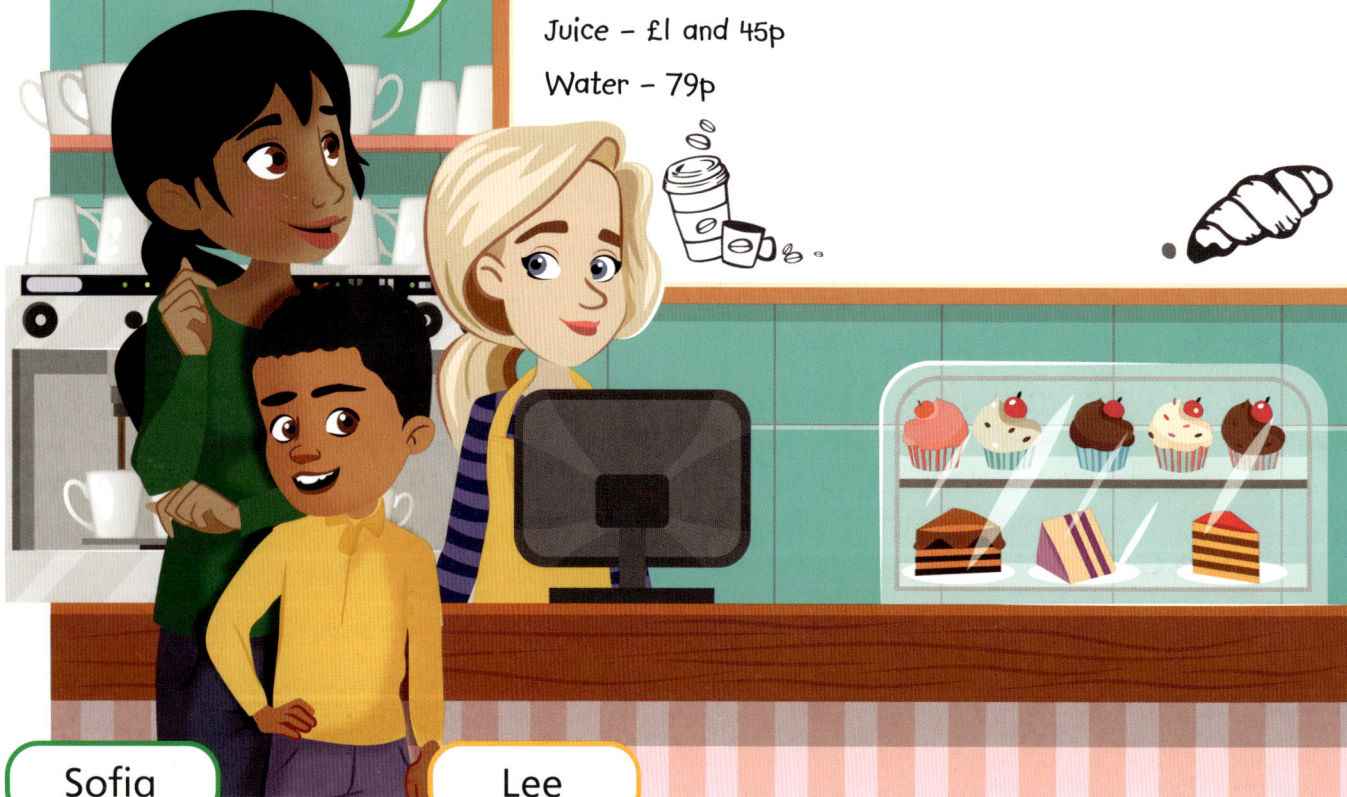

Sofia

Lee

1 **a)** How much do the tea and cake cost Sofia in total?

b) Lee wants juice and a toastie.

Change each amount into pence and then add to find the total.

52

Key 1p 2p 5p 10p 20p 50p £1 £2

Share

a) A cup of tea costs £1 and 20p.

A slice of cake costs £2 and 32p.

I made each amount with coins and added them together.

£1 and 20p   +   £2 and 32p   =   £3 and 52p

Add the pounds first: £1 + £2 = £3

Then add the pence: 20p + 32p = 52p

The tea and cake cost Sophia £3 and 52p in total.

b) £1 and 45p = 145p

£2 and 80p = 280p

	H	T	O
	1	4	5
+	2	8	0
	4	2	5
	1		

I changed each amount to pence and then did a column addition.

425p is the same as £4 and 25p.

The juice and toastie cost Lee £4 and 25p in total.

£5   £10   £20   £50

Think together

1 What is the total cost?

£2 and 20p

£3 and 58p

Add the pounds. £2 + £3 = £ ☐

Add the pence. 20p + 58p = ☐ p

The total cost is £ ☐ and ☐ p.

2 What is the total cost?

£1 and 80p

£1 and 45p

£1 and 80p = ☐ p

£1 and 45p = ☐ p

	H	T	O
		8	0
+	1	4	5

Key 1p 2p 5p 10p 20p 50p £1 £2

CHALLENGE

3 The tills show the cost of some items from the café.

Tea – £1 and 20p

Small coffee – £1 and 80p

Large coffee – £2 and 20p

Juice – £1 and 45p

Water – 79p

Toastie – £2 and 80p

Slice of cake – £2 and 32p

Strawberry tart – £3 and 58p

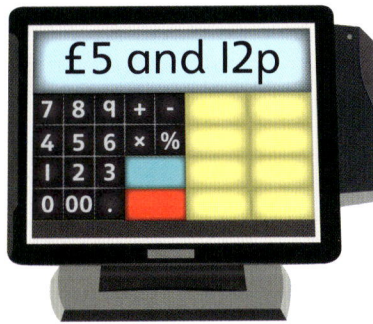

£1 and 99p	£5 and 12p	£8 and 10p
7 8 9 + -	7 8 9 + -	7 8 9 + -
4 5 6 × %	4 5 6 × %	4 5 6 × %
1 2 3	1 2 3	1 2 3
0 00 .	0 00 .	0 00 .

Work out which items were bought at each till.

I will use the end numbers to help me.

I wonder if anyone bought more than two items.

£5   £10   £20   £50

→ **Practice book 3C p38**

Subtract money

Discover

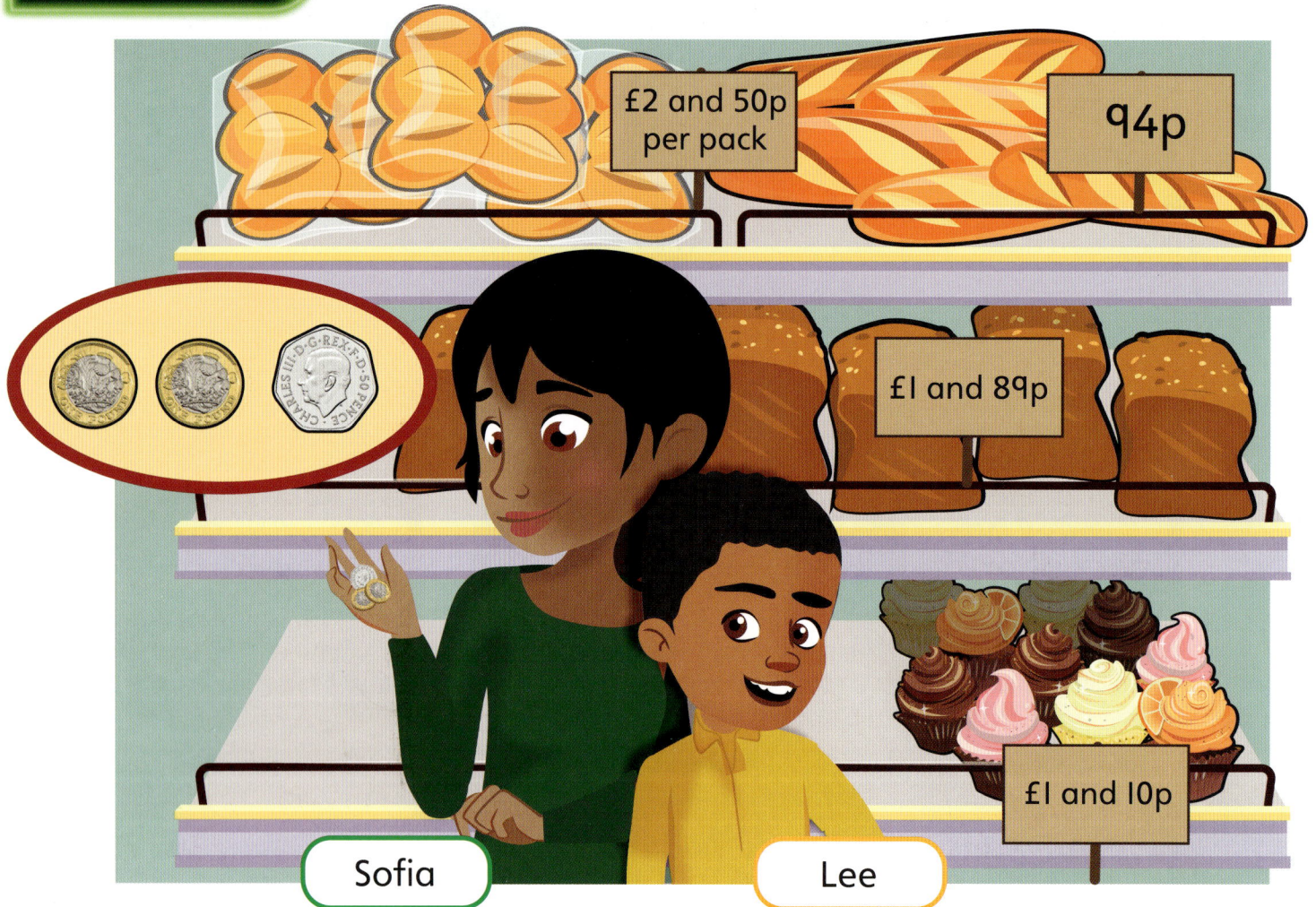

£2 and 50p per pack

94p

£1 and 89p

£1 and 10p

Sofia

Lee

1 **a)** Sofia buys a cupcake.

How much money does she have left?

b) How much cheaper is a loaf of bread than a pack of bread rolls?

Key 1p 2p 5p 10p 20p 50p £1 £2

Share

a) Sofia has £2 and 50p.

She buys a cupcake for £1 and 10p.

> I had to exchange the 50p for other coins.

Subtract £1 first.

Then subtract 10p.

Sofia has £1 and 40p left.

b) A loaf of bread costs £1 and 89p.

A pack of bread rolls costs £2 and 50p.

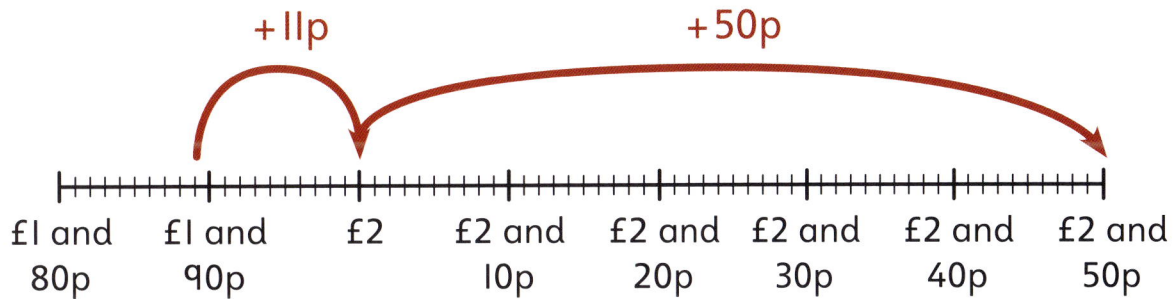

+11p   +50p

£1 and 80p | £1 and 90p | £2 | £2 and 10p | £2 and 20p | £2 and 30p | £2 and 40p | £2 and 50p

> To find the difference between the costs, I counted on.

H	T	O
^{1}2	^{1}4$\cancel{5}$	^{1}0
− 1	8	9
	6	1

> I changed the amounts to pence and used column subtraction.

11p + 50p = 61p

£2 and 50p − £1 and 89p = 61p

A loaf of bread is 61p cheaper than a pack of bread rolls.

£5   £10   £20   £50

57

Think together

1 How much more does a loaf of bread cost than a breadstick?

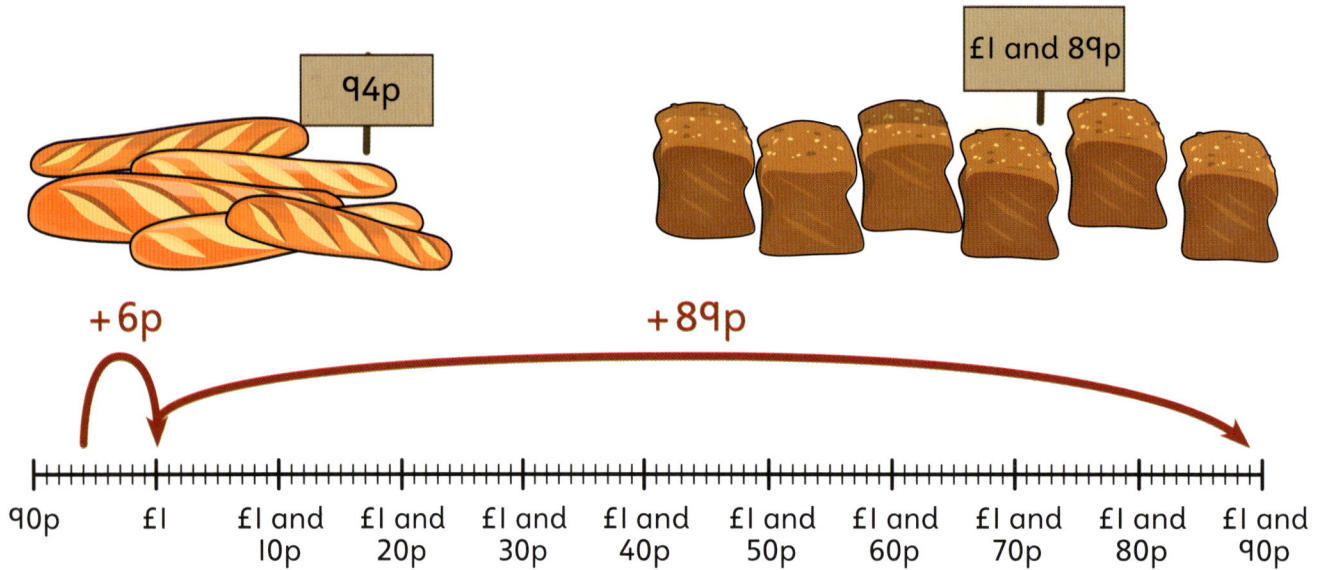

94p

£1 and 89p

+6p +89p

| 90p | £1 | £1 and 10p | £1 and 20p | £1 and 30p | £1 and 40p | £1 and 50p | £1 and 60p | £1 and 70p | £1 and 80p | £1 and 90p |

2 Lee has £5 and 42p.

He buys a custard tart.

How much money does Lee have left?

56p

Key 1p 2p 5p 10p 20p 50p £1 £2

CHALLENGE

3 **a)** Predict which of these subtractions will have an answer less than £1.

£1 and 95p – £1 and 42p

£5 and 30p – £1 and 50p

£2 and 18p – 64p

£4 and 45p – £3 and 88p

b) Work out the answers. Were your predictions correct?

I will subtract the pounds and pence separately.

If I change the amounts to pence I can do a column subtraction.

£5 £10 £20 £50

→ Practice book 3C p41

Find change

Discover

That will be £2 and 35p please.

Sofia

Lee

1 a) Sofia pays with a £5 note.

Count on to work out the change.

b) Check your answer by converting each amount to pence and then subtracting.

Key 1p 2p 5p 10p 20p 50p £1 £2

Share

a) The cost of the shopping is £2 and 35p.

Sofia pays with a £5 note.

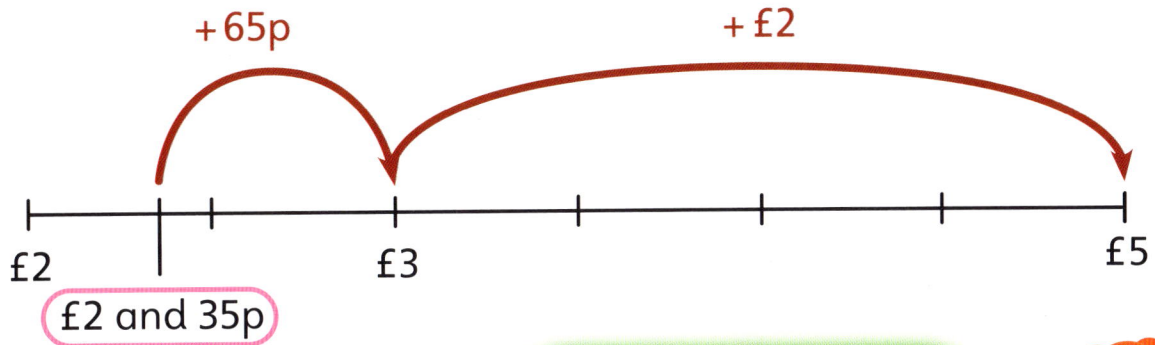

+65p   +£2

£2   £3   £5

£2 and 35p

> I added 65p to get to the next pound and then £2 to get to £5.

Sofia received £2 and 65p change.

b)

H	T	O
$^4\cancel{5}$	$^{9}\!/\!_{1}\cancel{0}$	$^1 0$
− 2	3	5
2	6	5

265p = £2 and 65p

Sofia received £2 and 65p change.

Think together

1. Work out the change for each amount.

a)

b)

2.

Holly

That will be £4 and 80p please.

Sofia

I will get £6 and 20p change from a £10 note.

Is Sofia correct?

Key 1p 2p 5p 10p 20p 50p £1 £2

CHALLENGE

3 Ambika buys a bar of chocolate with a £2 coin.

She receives this change.

How much did the bar of chocolate cost?

I will try to work out the coins I need to make £2. This will help me.

I wonder if I need to add or subtract.

£5   £10   £20   £50

→ Practice book 3C p44

End of unit check

1 How much money is shown here?

A £7 and 42p   **B** £742   **C** £6 and 42p   **D** £7 and 37p

2 What is 458p in pounds and pence?

A £4 and 58p   **B** £45 and 8p   **C** £458   **D** £4 and 85p

3 Which of the following sets of coins does not make £1?

A

B

C

D

Key 1p 2p 5p 10p 20p 50p £1 £2

4 How much money is shown here?

A   £6 and 87p   B   £7 and 87p   C   £787   D   87p

5 A sandwich cost £3 and 65p. Kate pays with .

How much change does Kate get?

A   £2 and 35p   B   £1 and 45p   C   £1 and 35p   D   £2 and 45p

6 Olivia wants to buy a new sports cap.

She has £4 and 20p.

Her mum gives her £5 and 90p.

Does she have enough to buy the sports cap?

£12 and 70p

£5   £10   £20   £50

→ Practice book 3C p47

Unit 13
Time

In this unit we will …

⚡ Learn about Roman numerals

⚡ Learn about hours, days, months and years

⚡ Estimate times

⚡ Tell the time to the nearest minute

⚡ Calculate start and end times

⚡ Solve time problems

Do you remember how to count the number of minutes past or to an o'clock time?

5 minutes

10 minutes

15 minutes

20 minutes

25 minutes

5 minutes

10 minutes

15 minutes

20 minutes

25 minutes

We will be using some maths words.
Do you recognise any of these?

numerals   month   year   midnight

midday   am   pm

duration   hour   minute

second   past   to

start   end   digital clock

How do you know
what the time is?

Roman numerals to 12

Discover

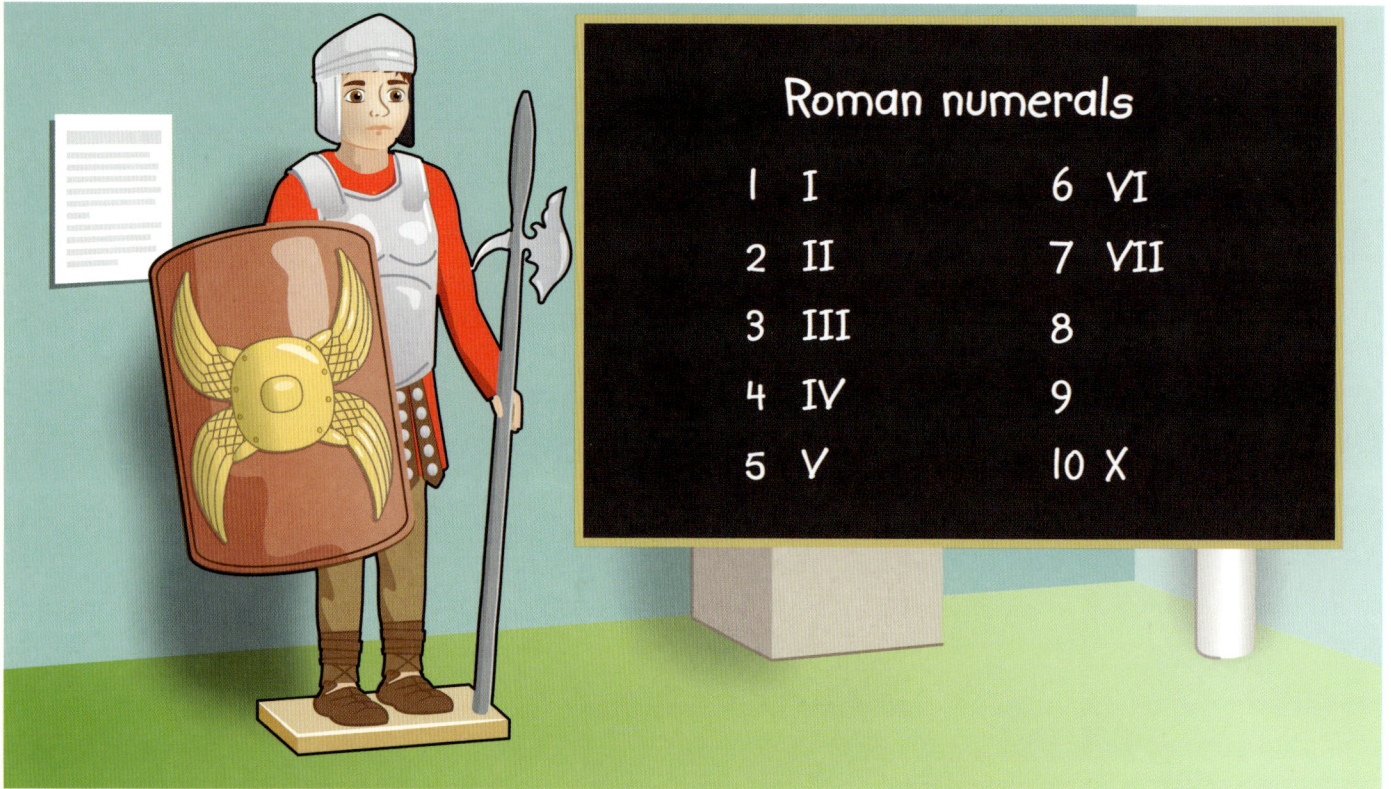

Roman numerals

1	I	6	VI
2	II	7	VII
3	III	8	
4	IV	9	
5	V	10	X

1 **a)** What do you think the Roman **numerals** are for 8 and 9?

b) Where might you see Roman numerals?

Share

a)

I saw that when 'I' appeared before V, this meant I less than 5. When 'I' appeared after V it meant I more than 5. I saw other patterns like this one.

VIII represents 8.

IX represents 9.

Roman numerals

I	I	6	VI
2	II	7	VII
3	III	8	VIII
4	IV	9	XI
5	V	10	X

b) Here are three places you might have seen Roman numerals.

clock faces   film or book titles   coins

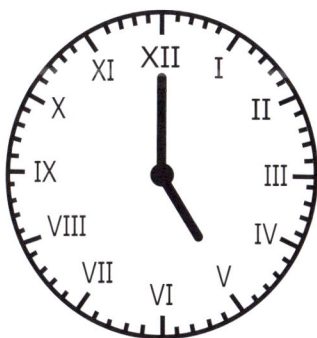

The Moonlight Saga: Episode VII

Think together

1 What number episodes are these?

a)

b)

2 What o'clock times are shown?

a)

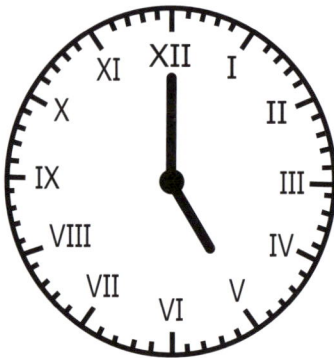

b)

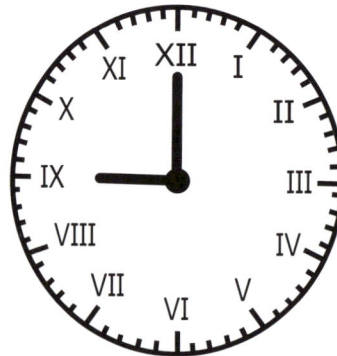

CHALLENGE

3 What times do the clocks show?

a)
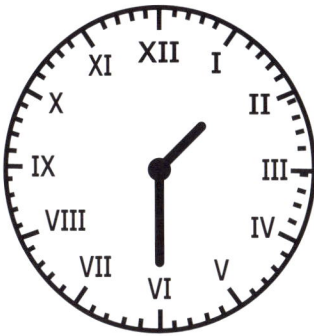

c)

b)
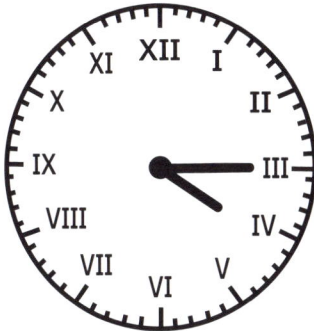

d)

When the minute hand points to 6 I think this tells me it is half past the hour.

I think some of these are 'past' times and some are 'to' times.

→ Practice book 3C p49

Tell the time to 5 minutes

Discover

1 a) How many minutes past 11 o'clock is it?

b) How many minutes to 12 o'clock is it?

Share

a) Look at the minute hand. It has moved past 11 numbers since 11 o'clock.

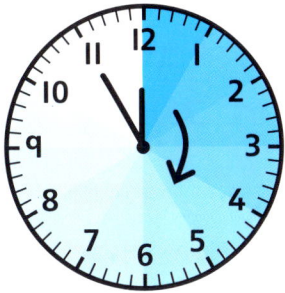

There are 5 minutes between each number on a clock.

11 × 5 = 55

It is 55 minutes past 11 o'clock.

b)

5 minutes to
10 minutes to
15 minutes to
20 minutes to
25 minutes to

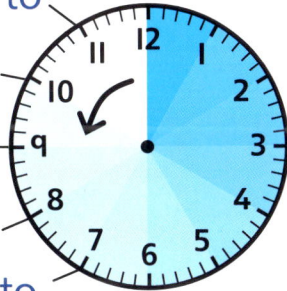

I counted back from an o'clock time to find the minutes to the next hour.

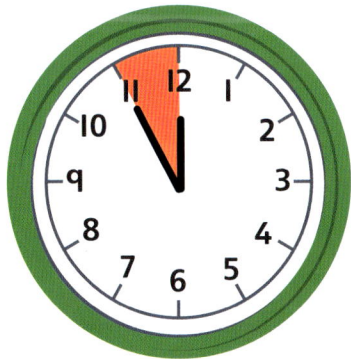

There are 5 minutes until 12 o'clock.

The time is 5 minutes to 12.

Think together

1 What times do the clocks show?

a)

c)

b)

I think counting in 5s is going to be useful here.

2 What time does the clock show?

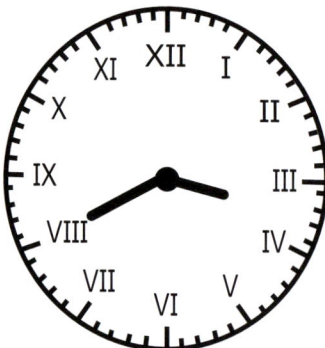

3 Use the clock to help you answer these questions.

CHALLENGE

a) Where might the minute and hour hands be if the time is 'something' past 6?

b) Where might the minute and hour hands be at 'something' to 10?

c) Where might the hands be if the time is twenty to 'something'?

I can say which half of the clock the minute hand is in.

I can say which two numbers the hour hand is pointing between.

75

→ Practice book 3C p52

Tell the time to the minute

Discover

I **a)** How many minutes past 10 o'clock was this photo taken?

b) Is there another way to say this time?

Share

a) There are 60 minutes in 1 hour.

I counted in jumps of 5s, and then 1s, to work out how many minutes past 10 o'clock it is.

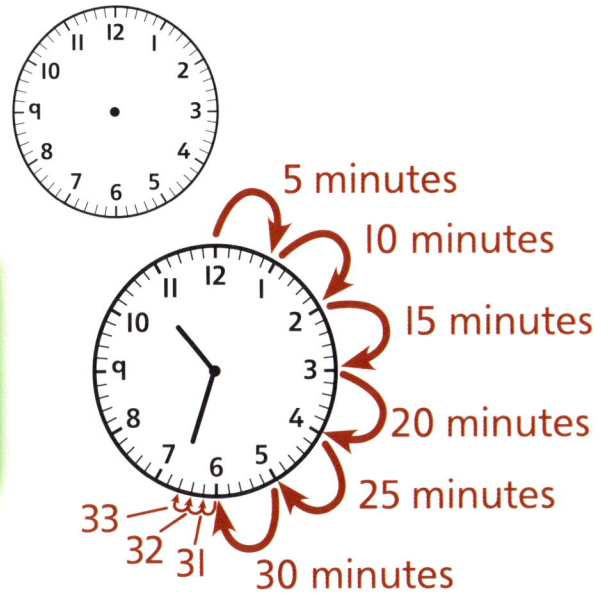

5 minutes
10 minutes
15 minutes
20 minutes
25 minutes
30 minutes
33
32 31

The photo was taken at 33 minutes past 10.

b) You can also count back from 11 o'clock.

5 minutes
10 minutes
15 minutes
20 minutes
25 minutes
26 27

I remembered that there are 60 minutes in 1 hour.

60 minutes − 33 minutes past 10 = 27 minutes to 11

Another way to say this time is 27 minutes to 11.

I did this as a subtraction.

Think together

1 What time does each clock show?

I will count in 5s and 1s.

a)

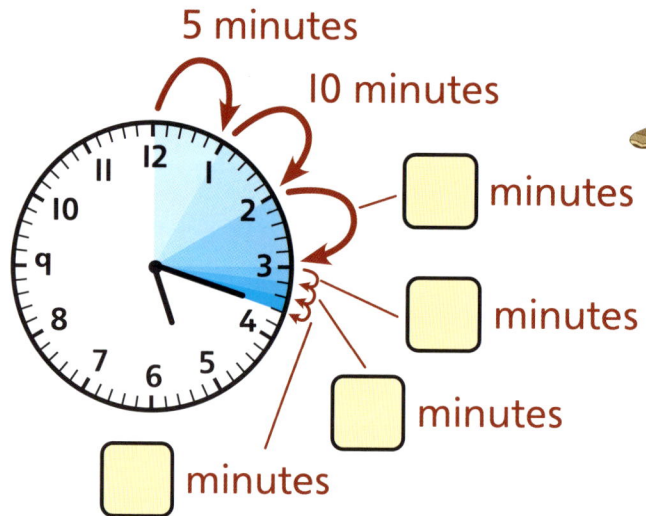

5 minutes

10 minutes

☐ minutes

☐ minutes

☐ minutes

☐ minutes

☐ minutes past 5

b)

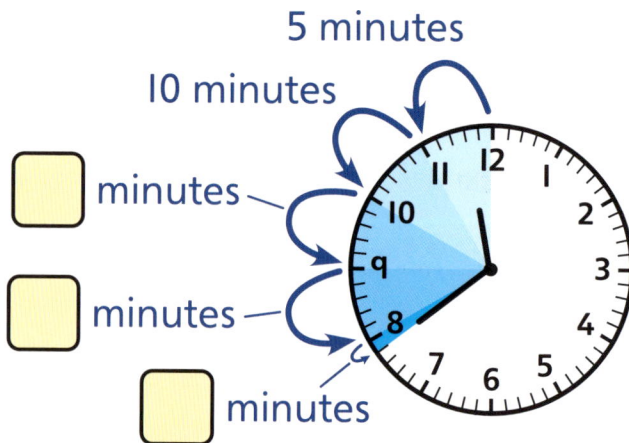

5 minutes

10 minutes

☐ minutes

☐ minutes

☐ minutes

☐ minutes to 12

2 What time is it?

a)

b)

c)
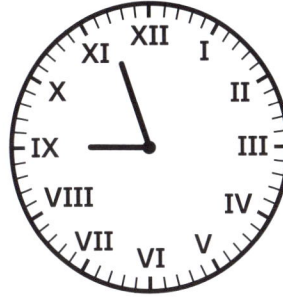

d)

a) ☐ minutes past 4

b) ☐ minutes to 5

c) ☐ minutes to ☐

d) ☐ minutes past ☐

3 This clock has no numbers on it.

Read the time to the nearest minute. Explain how you did it.

CHALLENGE

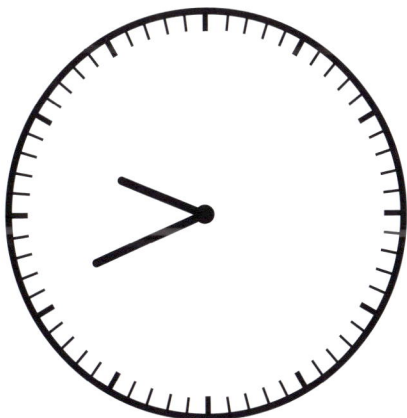

I can think of two ways to say this time.

79

→ Practice book 3C p55

Read time on a digital clock

Discover

My digital watch says eleven thirty-five.

11:35

1 **a)** What do you think the numbers mean on the **digital** watch?

b) Draw or make the time on an analogue clock.

How many minutes to the hour is it?

Share

a) The watch is digital.

II:35

The first number shows the hour.

The second number shows the number of minutes past the hour.

The time is 35 minutes past II.

b)

5 minutes
10 minutes
15 minutes
20 minutes
25 minutes
30 minutes
35 minutes

5 minutes
10 minutes
15 minutes
20 minutes
25 minutes

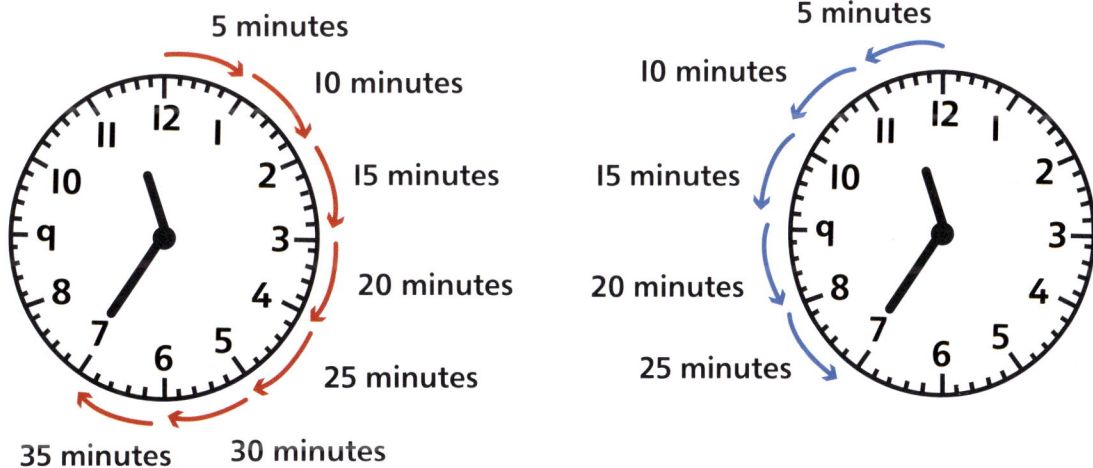

It is 25 minutes to 12.

Think together

1 Say these times using 'past the hour'.

a)

b)

c)

2 Convert these times from 'past the hour' to 'to the hour'.

a)

b)

CHALLENGE

3 Ebo wakes up and sees his alarm clock.

6:38 AM

It's 22 minutes to 7.

Ebo

a) Is Ebo correct?

I wonder how many minutes past 6 it is.

There are 60 minutes in an hour. If I know how many minutes past 6 it is, I can work out how many minutes until 7 o'clock.

b) Ebo goes back to sleep.

He wakes up at thirty-four minutes to 9.

What does his clock show?

83

→ Practice book 3C p58

Use am and pm

Discover

1 **a)** What time should the clock on the wall show?

b) Is it the morning or the evening?

How do you know?

Share

a)

I needed to remember what the numbers on the digital clock represent.

Remember, the first number shows the hour. The second number shows the number of minutes past that hour. This is always two digits.

8:54 am

The digital clock shows 54 minutes past 8.

We can also say this as '6 minutes to 9'.

The clock on the wall should show the time like this.

b) The letters 'am' and 'pm' show what time of day it is.

8:54 am

These letters come from Latin.

Ante meridiem **(am)** means before **midday** (from **midnight** until midday).

Post meridiem **(pm)** means after midday (from midday until midnight).

It is morning because the digital clock says 'am'.

Think together

1) **a)** Match the times.

b) Which clocks show times in the morning?

2 It is the evening.

Which digital clock shows the same time as the clock face?

A

C

B

D

3 How many minutes is it **to** the hour?

CHALLENGE

I think this shows minutes past the hour.

I can think of two ways to work it out.

87

→ Practice book 3C p61

Years, months and days

Discover

I **a)** How many months are in a year?

How many days are in each month?

b) How many days are in a year?

Share

a) There are 12 months in a year.

Look at the last day of each month. It shows how many days are in that month.

> A year is the time it takes for planet Earth to travel once around the Sun.

January	February	March	April
S M T W T F S	S M T W T F S	S M T W T F S	S M T W T F S
1 2 3 4 5 6	1 2 3	1 2 3	1 2 3 4 5 6 7
7 8 9 10 11 12 13	4 5 6 7 8 9 10	4 5 6 7 8 9 10	8 9 10 11 12 13 14
14 15 16 17 18 19 20	11 12 13 14 15 16 17	11 12 13 14 15 16 17	15 16 17 18 19 20 21
21 22 23 24 25 26 27	18 19 20 21 22 23 24	18 19 20 21 22 23 24	22 23 24 25 26 27 28
28 29 30 31	25 26 27 28	25 26 27 28 29 30 31	29 30

May	June	July	August
S M T W T F S	S M T W T F S	S M T W T F S	S M T W T F S
1 2 3 4 5	1 2	1 2 3 4 5 6 7	1 2 3 4
6 7 8 9 10 11 12	3 4 5 6 7 8 9	8 9 10 11 12 13 14	5 6 7 8 9 10 11
13 14 15 16 17 18 19	10 11 12 13 14 15 16	15 16 17 18 19 20 21	12 13 14 15 16 17 18
20 21 22 23 24 25 26	17 18 19 20 21 22 23	22 23 24 25 26 27 28	19 20 21 22 23 24 25
27 28 29 30 31	24 25 26 27 28 29 30	29 30 31	26 27 28 29 30 31

September	October	November	December
S M T W T F S	S M T W T F S	S M T W T F S	S M T W T F S
1	1 2 3 4 5 6	1 2 3	1
2 3 4 5 6 7 8	7 8 9 10 11 12 13	4 5 6 7 8 9 10	2 3 4 5 6 7 8
9 10 11 12 13 14 15	14 15 16 17 18 19 20	11 12 13 14 15 16 17	9 10 11 12 13 14 15
16 17 18 19 20 21 22	21 22 23 24 25 26 27	18 19 20 21 22 23 24	16 17 18 19 20 21 22
23 24 25 26 27 28 29	28 29 30 31	25 26 27 28 29 30	23 24 25 26 27 28 29
30			30 31

January, March, May, July, August, October and December have 31 days.

April, June, September and November have 30 days.

February has 28 days (29 days in a leap year).

> I used my knuckles to help me remember. The months on my knuckles have 31 days.

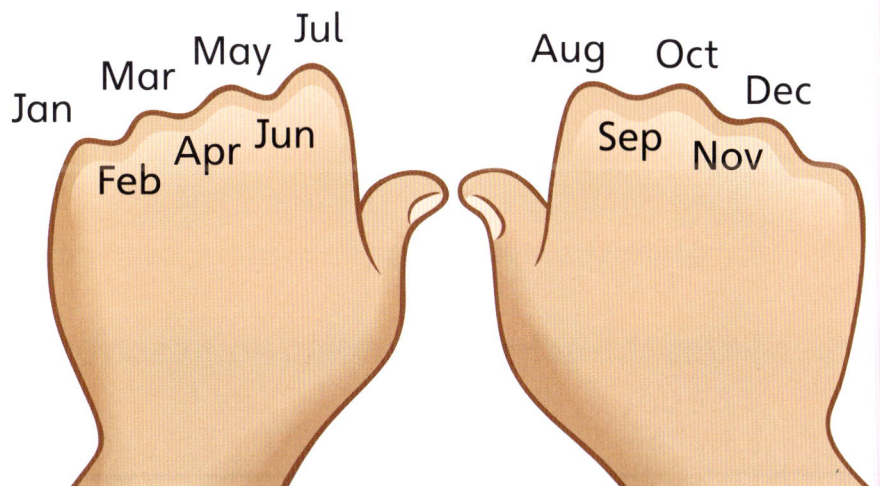

Jan Mar May Jul   Aug Oct Dec
Feb Apr Jun   Sep Nov

b) The number of days in each month helps us to find out how many days are in a whole year.

I month has 28 days.

4 months have 30 days: $4 \times 30 = 120$ days.

7 months have 31 days: $7 \times 31 = 217$ days.

$28 + 120 + 217 = 365$ days. There are 365 days in a year.

Think together

1

Some years are leap years. They have an extra day, which is 29 February.

a) Use the calendar to help you count on I week from 14 April. Count in days. 15 April is day I.

b) Use the calendar to help you count back 4 weeks from 30 July. Count in weeks.

2 **a)** How many days are in 5 weeks?

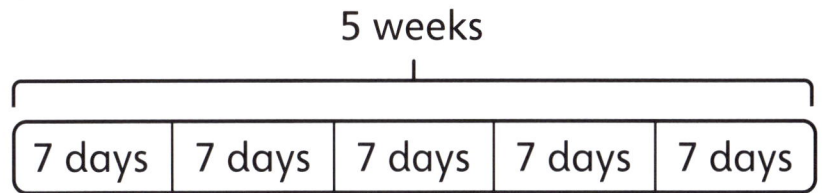

5 weeks

7 days	7 days	7 days	7 days	7 days

b) It is the 188th day of the year.

It is not a leap year.

How many days are left in the year?

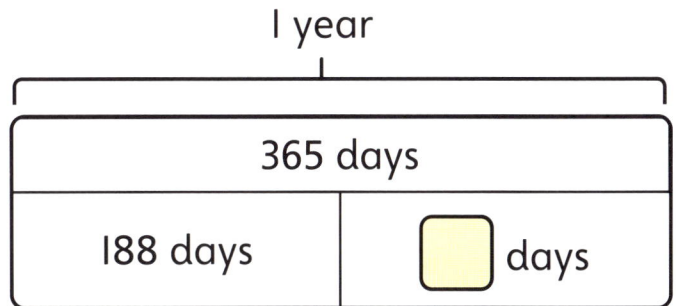

1 year

365 days	
188 days	☐ days

CHALLENGE

3 It takes nearly $365\frac{1}{4}$ days for the Earth to travel once around the Sun. This means the calendar needs to be adjusted every 4 years.

How do you think the calendar is adjusted for the extra quarter days?

We cannot have a quarter of a day at the **end** of a year. I think this has something to do with leap years.

365 days	$\frac{1}{4}$

365 days	$\frac{1}{4}$

365 days	$\frac{1}{4}$

365 days	$\frac{1}{4}$

→ Practice book 3C p64

Days and hours

Discover

When does a day start and end?

I think a day starts when the sun comes up and ends when it gets dark.

I think a day starts when I wake up and ends when I go to bed.

I think a day starts at midnight and ends at midnight the next day.

1 **a)** When does a day start and end?

b) How many hours are there in 1 day?

Share

a)

midnight   midday   midnight

| 12 | 1 | 2 | 3 | 4 | 5 | 6 | 7 | 8 | 9 | 10 | 11 | 12 | 1 | 2 | 3 | 4 | 5 | 6 | 7 | 8 | 9 | 10 | 11 | 12 |

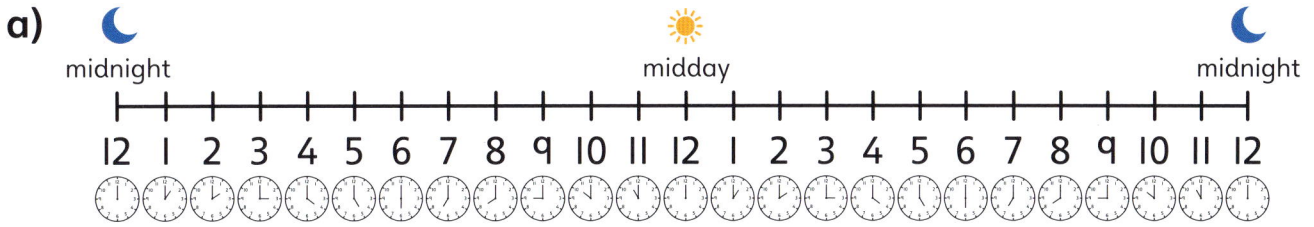

The start of the day is 12 o'clock at night. This is called midnight.

The middle of the day is 12 o'clock midday, or noon.

The end of the day is the next midnight. This is when a new day starts.

> I wonder if it can really be the start of a new day at midnight, even though it is dark.

> We start counting the 24 hours in a day at midnight.
>
> The day lasts until the next midnight, when we start the count again.

b) There are 12 hours from midnight until midday.

There are another 12 hours from midday until the next midnight.

$12 + 12 = 24$

There are 24 hours in 1 day.

Think together

1. Tim is thinking of some questions.

   Help Tim answer these questions.

   I wonder how many hours there are from 12 noon to 12 midnight.

   I wonder how many hours there are in 2 days.

   I wonder how many times the hour hand goes around the clock in a full day.

   Tim

2. a) How many hours are there from 7 pm until the end of the day?

   b) How many hours are there from 7 am until the end of the day?

3 This is what Emma does in a day.

9 hours   7 hours   3 hours

How much time does Emma have left in the day to do other things?

I will think about my own day and the number of hours in the day I spend doing different things.

I don't play sports for as long as Emma does, but I sleep a bit longer than she does.

95

→ Practice book 3C p67

Hours and minutes – start and end times

Discover

2:47 pm

TICKETS

Olivia

BIG WHEEL
QUEUING TIME:

30 minutes

Max

DODGEMS
QUEUING TIME:

6 minutes

CAROUSEL
QUEUING TIME:

14 minutes

I want to go on the big wheel at twenty-five past 4.

1 **a)** Max has just started queuing for the dodgems. At what time will he get on?

b) When should Olivia start queuing for the big wheel?

Share

a)

I used the start time and the **duration** to help me find the end time.

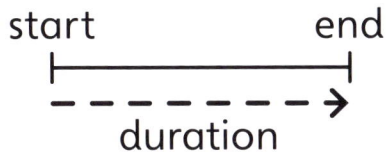

Start + Duration = End

 + **DODGEMS QUEUING TIME: 6 minutes** =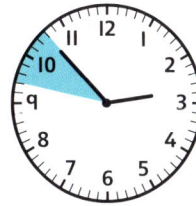

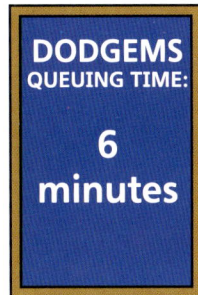

2:47 pm   2:53 pm

The time is now 2:47 pm.

47 + 6 = 53

Max will get on the dodgems at 2:53 pm.

b)

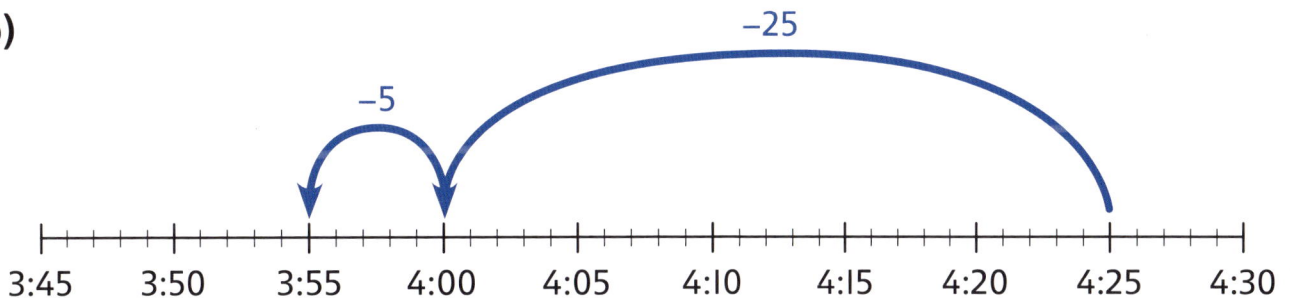

Olivia should start queuing for the big wheel at 3:55 pm.

Think together

CAROUSEL
QUEUING TIME:

14 minutes

1 It is 4:36 pm. If Max and Olivia start queuing now, at what time can they go on the carousel?

Start time

4:36 pm

2 The time now is 10:09 am.

Luis has been queuing for 25 minutes.

At what time did he start queuing?

End time

CHALLENGE

3 **a)** The queue for the helter-skelter takes 12 minutes.

Bella began queuing at 8 minutes to 3.

At what time will she go on the ride?

```
├──┼──┼──┼──╂──┼──┼──┼──╂──┼──┼──┼──╂──┼──┼──┼──╂──┼──┼──┼──╂──┼──┼──┼──╂──┼──┼──┤
2:45      2:50      2:55      3:00      3:05      3:10      3:15
```

b) The journey home takes 59 minutes.

If the Khan family leave at 5:35 pm, what time will they get home?

Explain your method.

I wonder if there are different ways to find the answers to these questions.

→ Practice book 3C p70

Hours and minutes – durations

Discover

4:23 pm

4:51 pm

5:19 pm

1 **a)** How long does it take the farmer to plough the field?

b) When he has finished, how many more minutes go by before he has a cup of tea?

Share

a) The time something takes is called its duration.

I counted on from the start time until I reached the end time.

Start time + Duration = End time

4:00 pm   4:30 pm   5:00 pm

It takes the farmer 28 minutes to plough the field.

b)

+ 9 minutes   + 19 minutes

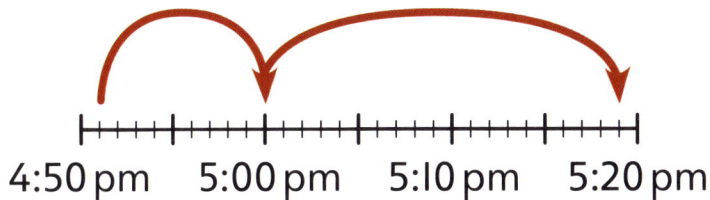

I used a number line to find the answer.

9 + 19 = 28 minutes

Another 28 minutes go by before the farmer has a cup of tea.

Think together

1 A farmer starts milking the cows at 5:13 am.

She finishes at 5:57 am.

How long does it take?

5:00 5:05 5:10 5:15 5:20 5:25 5:30 5:35 5:40 5:45 5:50 5:55 6:00

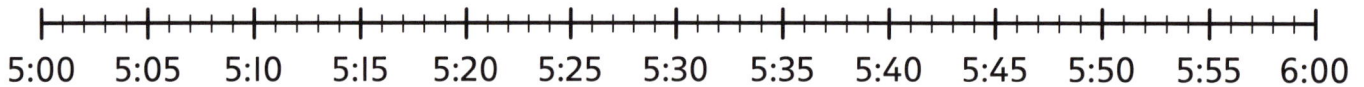

2 A lorry driver arrives at a farm to collect vegetables at 35 minutes past 2 in the afternoon.

He leaves at 22 minutes past 3.

How long was he at the farm for?

2:35 PM

I will draw the clock faces and use them to work out the duration.

I always draw a number line to calculate how long something takes.

3

CHALLENGE

I started collecting the eggs at 4:32 pm. I finished at 5:55 pm.

How long did it take the farmer to collect all the eggs?

Show two ways of finding the answer.

I will try counting on.

I wonder if there is a quicker way when the answer will be more than 1 hour.

→ Practice book 3C p73

Hours and minutes – compare durations

Discover

OPEN DAY!
MORNING

Meet the Author
9:06 am – 10:00 am

Songs and Stories
11:35 am – 12:20 pm

Poetry Workshop
1:40 pm – 2:40 pm

1 a) How long does each activity last?

   b) Which activity lasts the longest?

Share

Remember, 60 minutes make 1 hour.

a)

Meet the Author:
9:06 am to 10:00 am
= 54 minutes

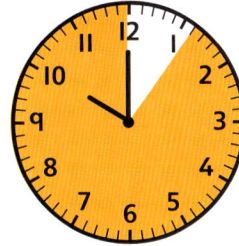

+ 54 minutes

Songs and Stories:
11:35 am to 12:20 pm
= 45 minutes

+ 25 minutes   + 20 minutes

25 + 20 = 45 minutes

Poetry Workshop:
1:40 pm to 2:40 pm
= 60 minutes

+ 60 minutes

I showed the number of minutes on a number line.

Songs and Stories   Meet the Author   Poetry Workshop

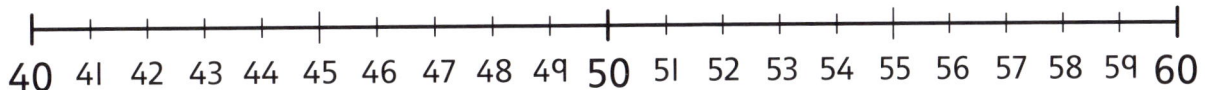

40 41 42 43 44 45 46 47 48 49 50 51 52 53 54 55 56 57 58 59 60

b)

45 minutes < 54 minutes   54 minutes < 60 minutes

The Poetry Workshop activity lasts the longest.

Think together

1 Here are the times for two library events. Which event lasts longer?

Story Time

4:40 pm   5:09 pm

Make a Book

4:45 pm   5:11 pm

The second event starts 5 minutes later than the first event. I can use this to help me see which lasts longer.

2 Which of these durations is the longest?

A

B

C

from 8:12 am
until 8:48 am

from 8:43 am
until 8:57 am

from 8:28 am
until 9:03 am

3 Order these durations, from shortest time to longest time.

CHALLENGE

A   from 4:28 pm until 5:35 pm

B   64 minutes

C   1 hour and 5 minutes

D   from 4:37 pm until 5:40 pm

I am going to work out A and D to start with.

Changing all the times into minutes might help me to compare them.

107

→ **Practice book 3C p76**

Minutes and seconds

Discover

1 **a)** How long have Richard and Amelia been playing?

b) What else could Lee use to measure time in seconds?

Share

a) Seconds are used to measure short periods of time.

60 seconds = I minute

I second is about the length of time it takes to say 'I second'!

Richard has been playing for 50 seconds.

Amelia has been playing for 35 seconds.

b) The thin red hand counts round the clock in seconds.

I knew that each mark on the clock face shows I second.

Lee could measure seconds using the clock on the wall, by counting the marks as the second hand moves.

Think together

1 How long does each activity take?

a)

Star jumps

Start time

End time

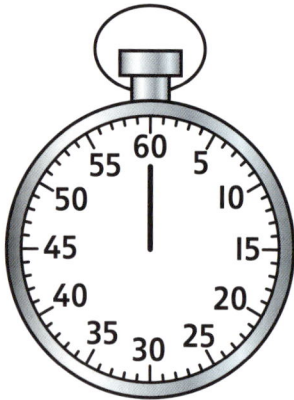  

b)

Running

Start time

End time

2 48 seconds have gone by.

How many seconds are left until a minute has passed?

I minute = 60 seconds	
48 seconds	?

3 How would you write each time in seconds?

CHALLENGE

a) $\frac{1}{2}$ a minute = ☐ seconds

b) $1\frac{1}{2}$ minutes = ☐ seconds

c) $2\frac{1}{2}$ minutes = ☐ seconds

I am going to use what I know about the number of seconds in a whole minute to help me.

III

→ Practice book 3C p79

Solve problems with time

Discover

① **a)** Which will take longer to fill, the jug or the bath?

b) What unit of time would you use to measure how long it takes to fill the jug and the bath?

Share

a) It will take longer to fill the bath than the jug as the bath has a greater capacity.

> I saw that the bath would hold more water than the jug so it would take longer to fill.

b)

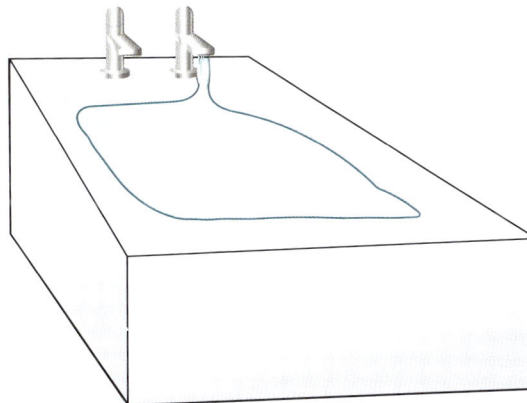

I would use seconds to measure how long it takes to fill the jug,

I would use minutes and seconds to measure how long it takes to fill the bath.

Think together

1 Choose the most appropriate unit for measuring the duration of each.

| seconds | minutes | hours | days | years |

The time it takes to play a football game.

The time it takes to fly to the moon.

The time it takes to blow up a balloon.

The time it takes for a tree to grow tall.

2 It takes Ambika 18 seconds to run a race.

It takes Aki 25 seconds to run the same race.

Is Aki correct?

I won the race because my time is greater.

Aki

CHALLENGE

3 Emma and Max are both going to the seaside.

I will use minutes to measure the time it takes me to get to the seaside.

Emma

I will use hours to measure the time it takes me.

Max

Explain how it is possible for Emma and Max to use different units of time to measure their journeys.

I wonder if it is to do with where they live.

I will use my knowledge of how many minutes are in 1 hour to help me explain.

→ **Practice book 3C p82**

End of unit check

1 One of these months has 30 days. Which is it?

A January

B February

C March

D April

2 Which one of these statements is not true?

A There are 12 months in a year.

B A day lasts from the time you get up to the time you go to bed.

C A day lasts 24 hours.

D A year usually lasts 365 days. Sometimes it lasts 366 days.

3 This clock shows an afternoon time. What time is it?

A 4:58 am

B 2 minutes to 5 am

C 4:58 pm

D 24 minutes past 11

4 It is 10:47 pm. The duration of a TV programme is 33 minutes. What time will it finish?

A twenty past 11 at night

B 10:80 pm

C twenty past 10 at night

D 11:20 am

5 Molly is timing $1\frac{1}{2}$ minutes. How many seconds is this?

A 60 seconds

B 90 seconds

C $60\frac{1}{2}$ seconds

D $1\frac{1}{2}$ seconds

6 A train starts its journey at this time in the morning.

It finishes its journey at this time in the afternoon.

How long is the train journey?

➔ **Practice book 3C p85**

Unit 14
Angles and properties of shapes

In this unit we will ...
- ⚡ Learn about turns
- ⚡ Learn what a right angle is
- ⚡ Understand and draw parallel and perpendicular lines
- ⚡ Identify and draw vertical and horizontal lines
- ⚡ Recognise and describe right angles and parallel and perpendicular lines in 2D shapes
- ⚡ Recognise, describe and construct 3D shapes

We will see some different 2D shapes. Which of these are quadrilaterals?

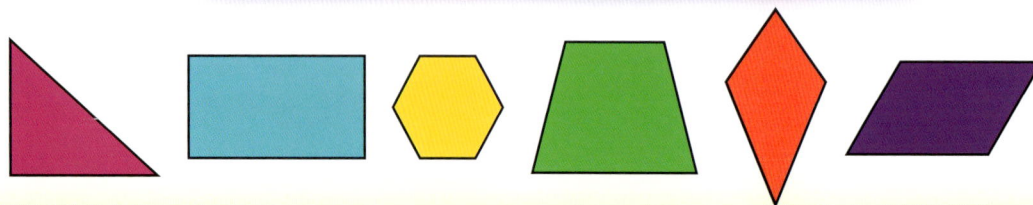

We will need some maths words.
Which of these have you heard before?

right angle · acute · obtuse · parallel · perpendicular · vertical · horizontal · triangle · quadrilateral · kite · trapezium · rhombus · parallelogram · cuboid · triangular prism · square-based pyramid · cone · tetrahedron · cylinder · sphere · edges · faces · vertices · clockwise · anticlockwise

We will look at 3D shapes too. Can you match the names to all these shapes?

cylinder · cone · square-based pyramid · sphere

 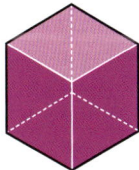 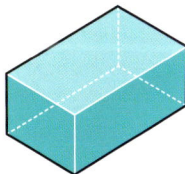 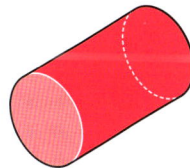

 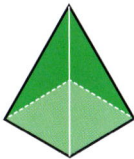 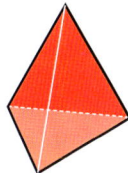 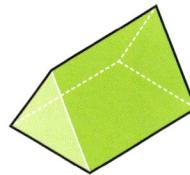

cube · triangular prism · cuboid · tetrahedron

Turns and angles

Discover

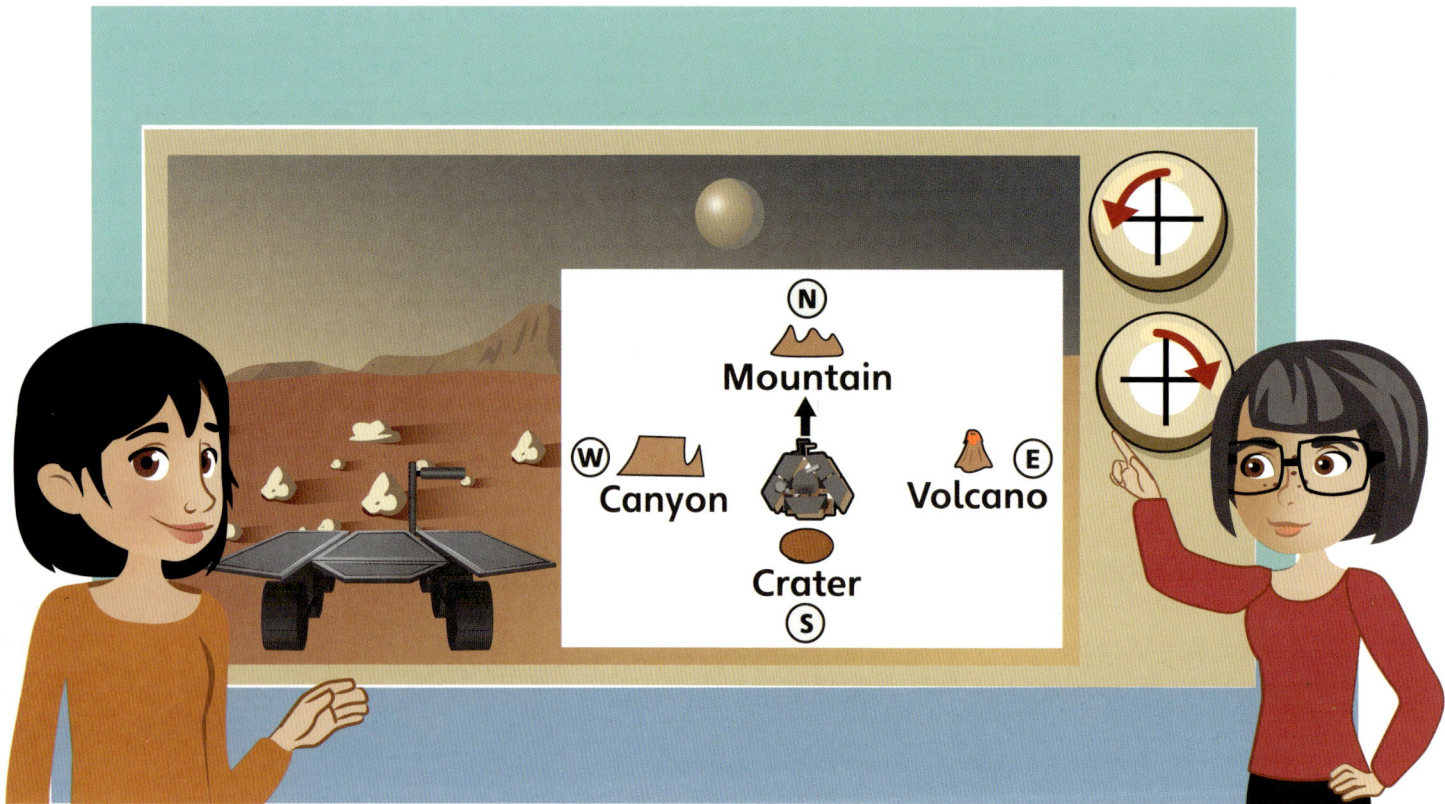

1 **a)** What do these buttons do?

b) What instruction will make the rover face the canyon?

Share

a) The buttons are for quarter turns.

anticlockwise

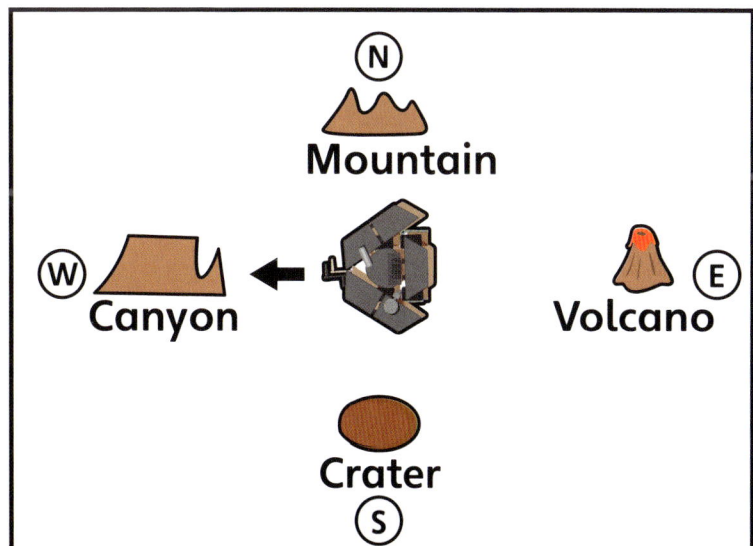

clockwise

A quarter turn is called a **right angle**. These are both right-angle turns.

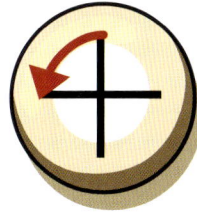

Anticlockwise and clockwise turn in opposite directions.

b) To face the canyon, the rover needs to make a quarter turn in the anticlockwise direction.

anticlockwise

N
Mountain

W
Canyon

E
Volcano

Crater
S

Think together

1 Now the rover faces the volcano.

    a) What would it face after a right-angle turn clockwise?

    b) What would it face after a right-angle turn anticlockwise?

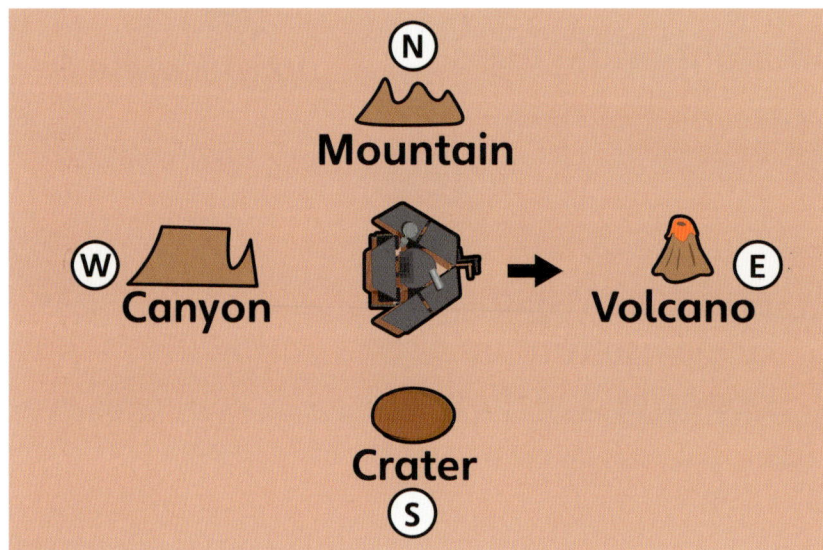

2 **a)** What would the rover face after a right-angle turn clockwise?

    b) What would it face after a right-angle turn anticlockwise?

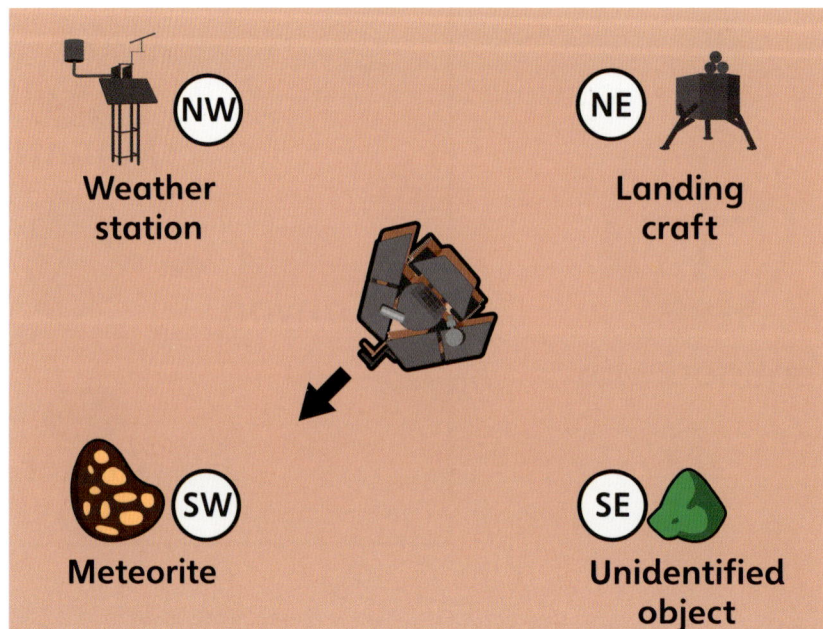

CHALLENGE

3 Look at this shape drawn on a piece of paper.

a) Draw this shape after one right-angle turn clockwise.

b) Draw this shape after two right-angle turns clockwise.

c) Draw this shape after three right-angle turns clockwise.

d) Draw this shape after four right-angle turns clockwise.

This reminds me of adding fractions.
$\frac{1}{4} + \frac{1}{4} = \frac{2}{4}$ which is equal to $\frac{1}{2}$.
$\frac{1}{4} + \frac{1}{4} + \frac{1}{4} + \frac{1}{4} = 1$

I will try this by drawing my own shape on a piece of paper and turning the piece of paper a quarter turn each time.

→ Practice book 3C p88

Right angles in shapes

Discover

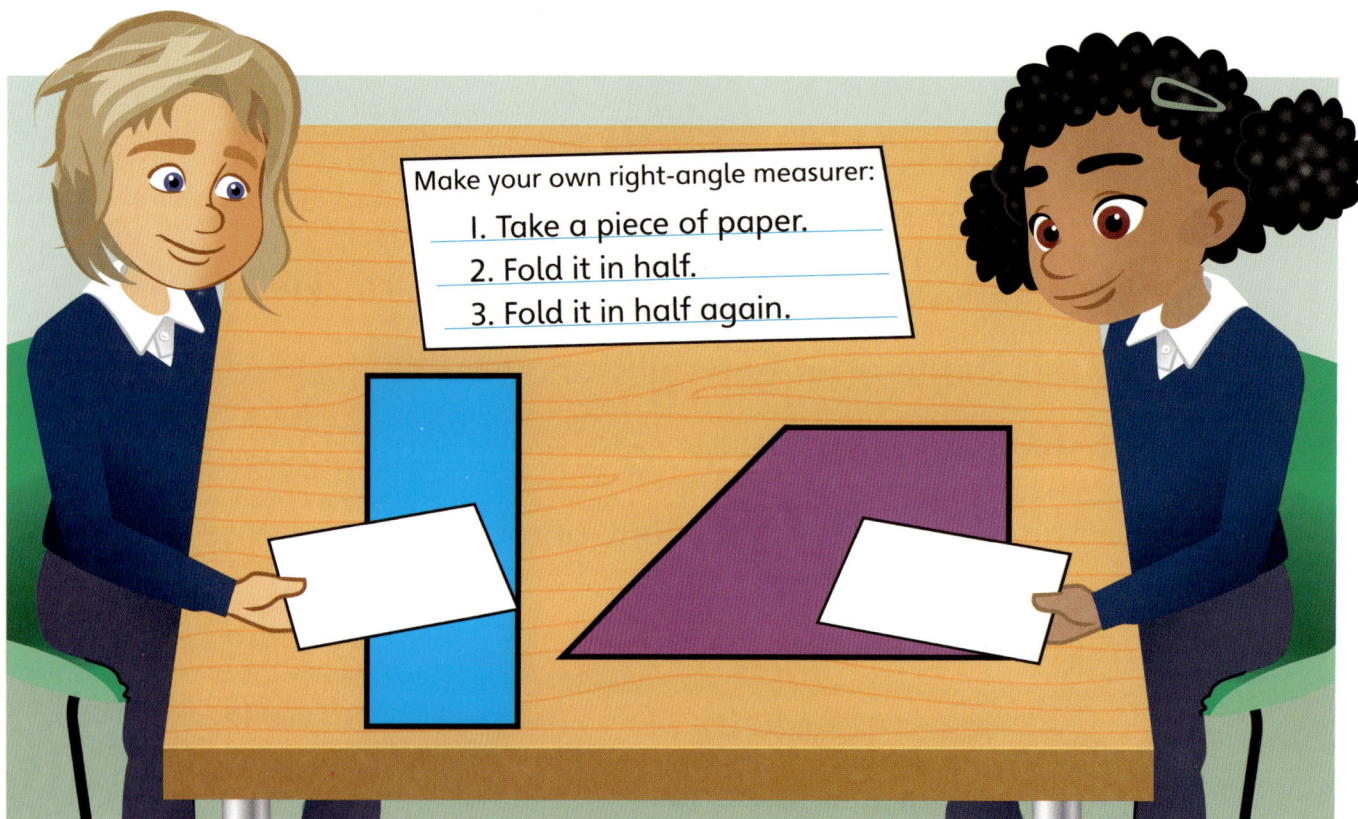

Make your own right-angle measurer:
1. Take a piece of paper.
2. Fold it in half.
3. Fold it in half again.

1 **a)** Make your own right-angle measurer.

Mark the right angle clearly.

b) Use your measurer to find any right angles in the two shapes.

Share

a)

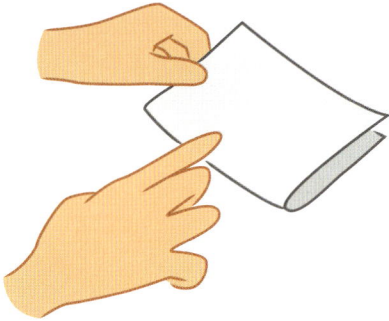

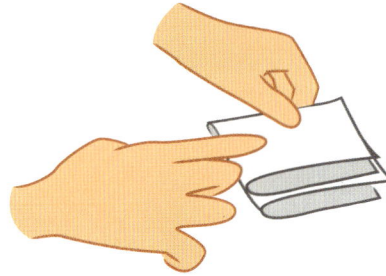

Where two folds meet, there is a right angle.

You can check a right angle by making a measurer.

A right angle is shown by a small square in the angle.

b)

I wonder what other shapes have 4 right angles.

4 right angles

2 right angles

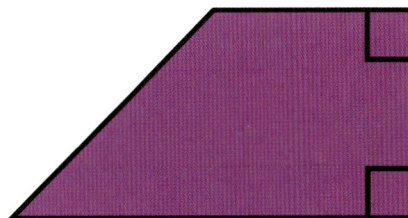

Think together

1 How many right angles are on this sports field?

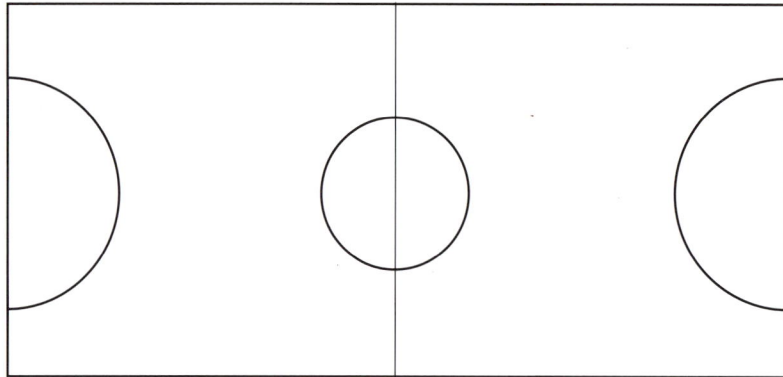

This has some curved lines. I do not know about angles in curves.

We only measure angles between straight lines.

2 How many right angles does each shape have?

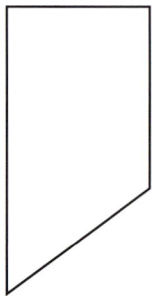
A

B

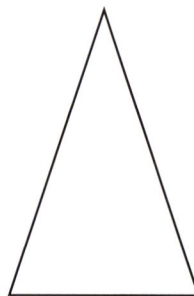
C

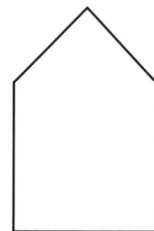
D

3 Help Dexter to decide if all the angles in the shape are right angles.

I cannot decide if one of these angles is a right angle or a three-quarter turn.

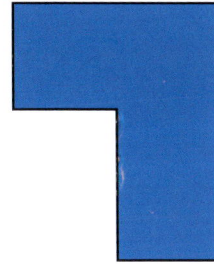

CHALLENGE

4 How could you draw a line along the dots to make a right angle with each line? Show a partner where you would draw your line.

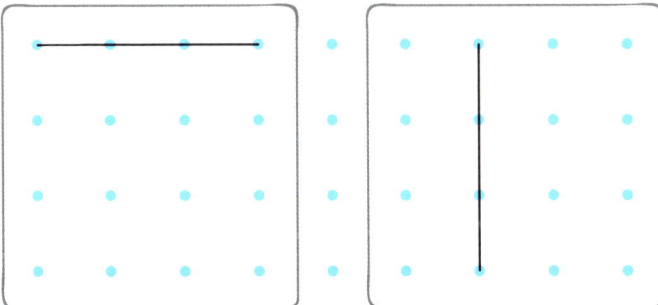

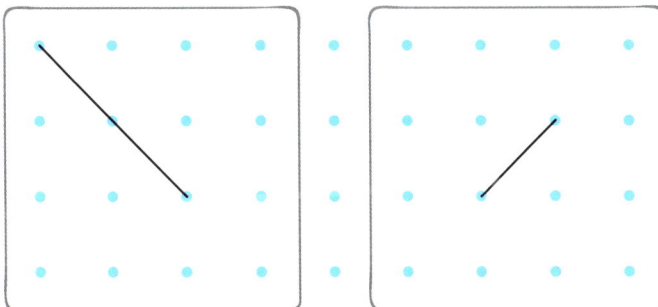

To complete the drawings, I need to draw a line that is at right angles to the line provided.

127

→ **Practice book 3C p91**

Compare angles

Discover

The best roof for snowy or rainy countries has an angle less than a right angle at its peak.

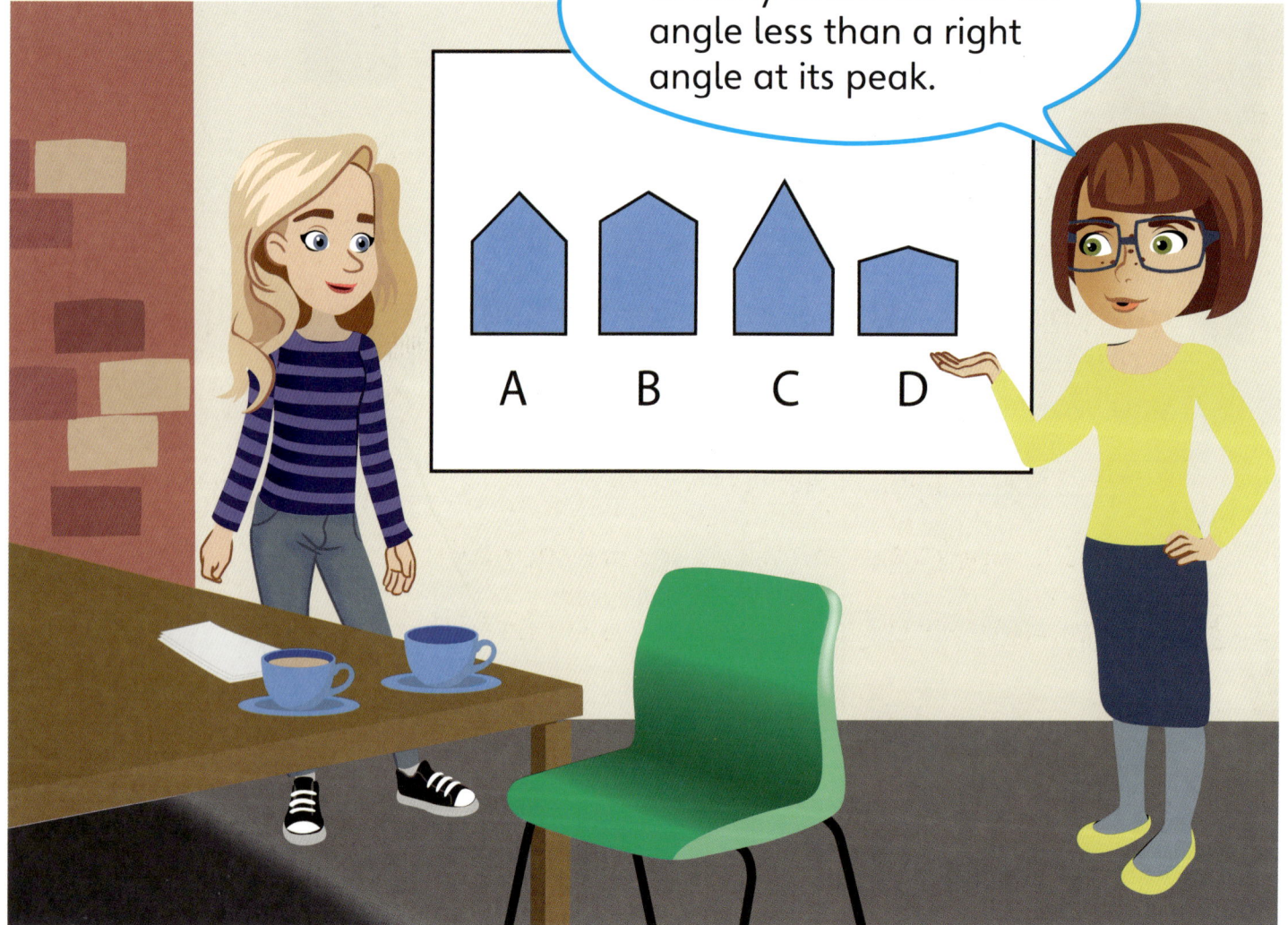

A   B   C   D

1 a) Which house would be good in a snowy country?

b) For countries with little rain, the angle at the peak of the roof is usually greater than a right angle. Would any of these houses suit a dry country?

Share

a)

I checked if the angles were greater than or less than a right angle.

I used a right-angle measurer and thought about turns.

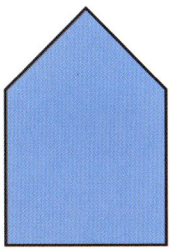 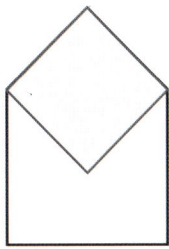 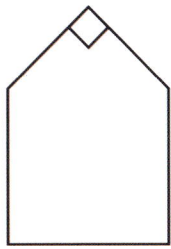 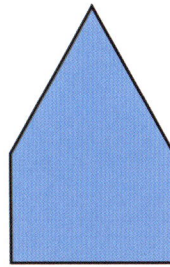 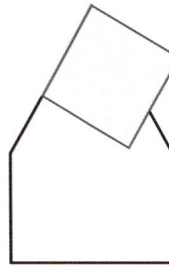 

A   C

Roof A is a right angle.

Roof C is less than a right angle.

House C would be good in a snowy country.

b) These roofs have angles greater than a right angle.

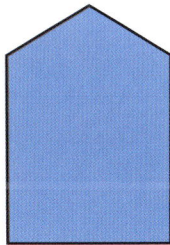 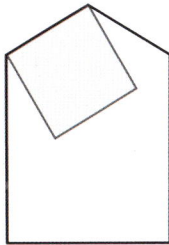 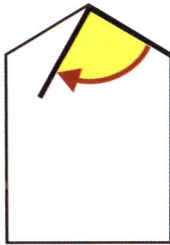   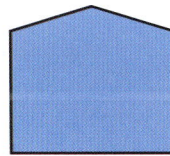 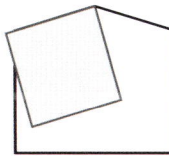 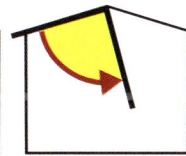

B   D

Roof B is greater than a right angle.

Roof D is greater than a right angle.

Houses B and D would suit a dry country.

Think together

1 Use a right-angle measurer to find out if each angle is greater than, equal to or less than a right angle.

A
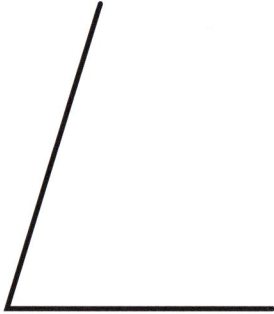

C

E
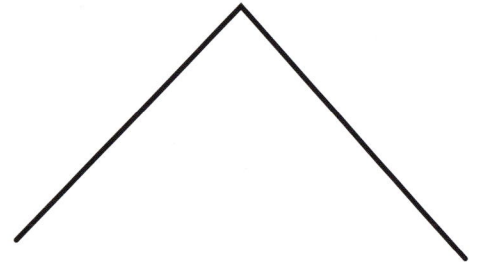

B
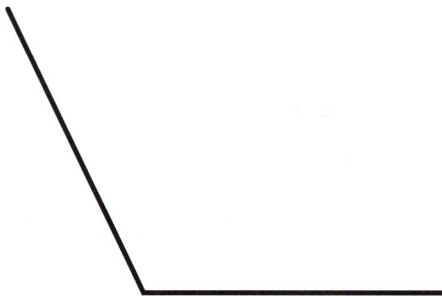

D
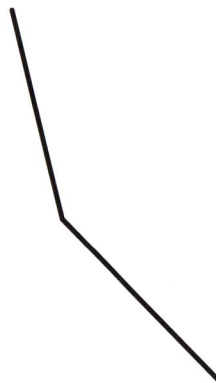

F
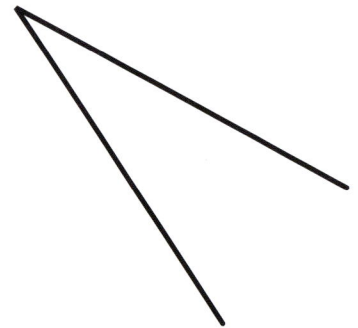

In maths, **acute** means less than a right angle, and **obtuse** means greater than a right angle.

2 Compare each angle with a right angle.

A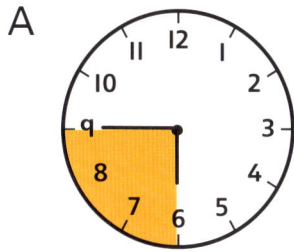

C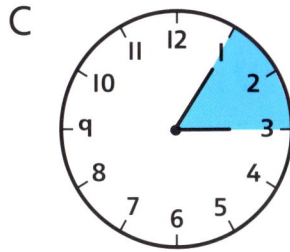

E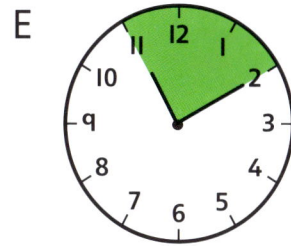

B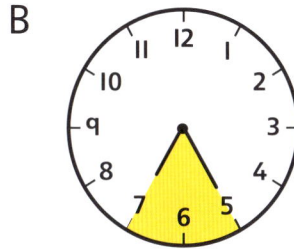

D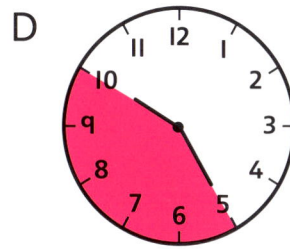

F

I know the angle between 12 and 3 is a right angle. I wonder which other pairs of numbers make a right angle.

3 Isla has made some angles. She wants to make some different acute and obtuse angles.
How many different acute and obtuse angles can Isla make?

CHALLENGE

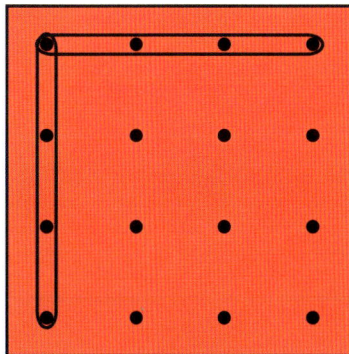

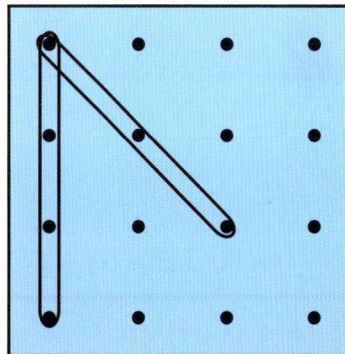

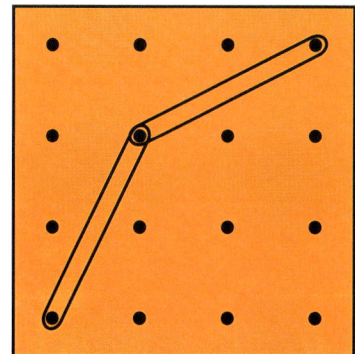

131

→ Practice book 3C p94

Measure and draw accurately

Discover

Kate: To make a 10 cm square I need to measure 10 cm across the top of the paper with my ruler.

Richard: I will measure along the top and the bottom.

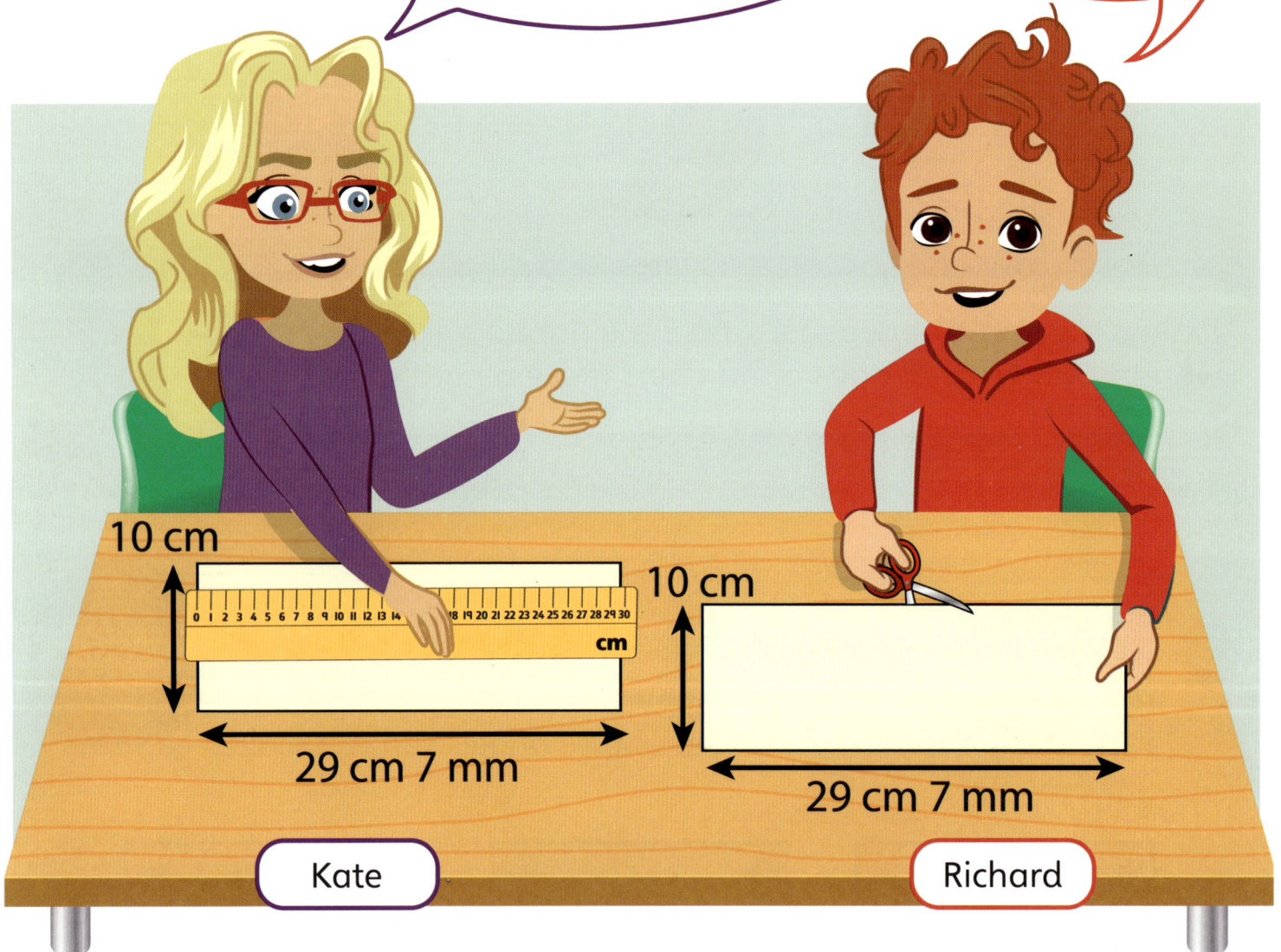

10 cm

0 1 2 3 4 5 6 7 8 9 10 11 12 13 14 18 19 20 21 22 23 24 25 26 27 28 29 30   cm

29 cm 7 mm

Kate

10 cm

29 cm 7 mm

Richard

1 **a)** Start with a strip of paper like this.
Measure and cut out 10 cm squares from the strip of paper.

b) What shape are you left with at the end?

Share

a) Measure 10 cm along the top and along the bottom. Mark 10 cm exactly.

10 cm

10 cm

10 cm

19 cm 7 mm

Line up a ruler to **both** marks. Place the pencil on one of the marks to help line up the ruler.

Draw a line to join the two marks. Then cut carefully along the line.

Repeat with the piece that remains.

10 cm

10 cm

9 cm 7 mm

You can make two 10 cm squares.

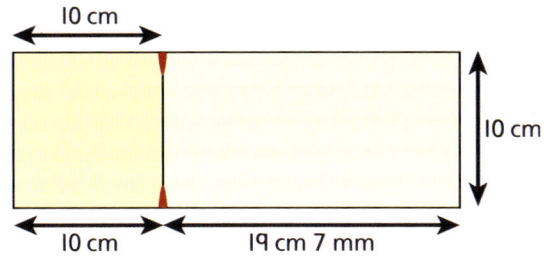

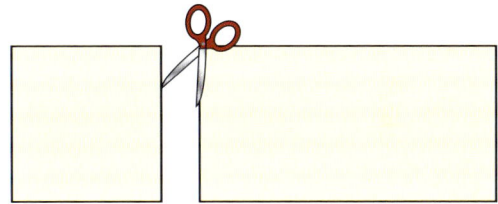

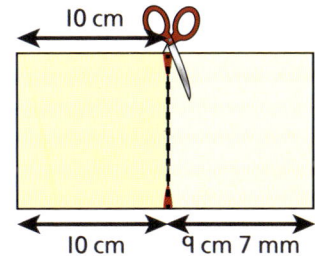

b) The whole strip was 29 cm and 7 mm wide.

20 cm have been cut away.

29 cm – 20 cm = 9 cm

The piece of paper left over is 9 cm and 7 mm wide. It is a rectangle because it is 10 cm tall and 9 cm 7 mm wide.

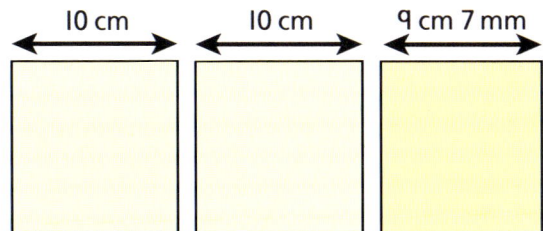

10 cm

10 cm

9 cm 7 mm

133

Think together

1 **a)** Draw these lines on one of the 10 cm squares you have made.

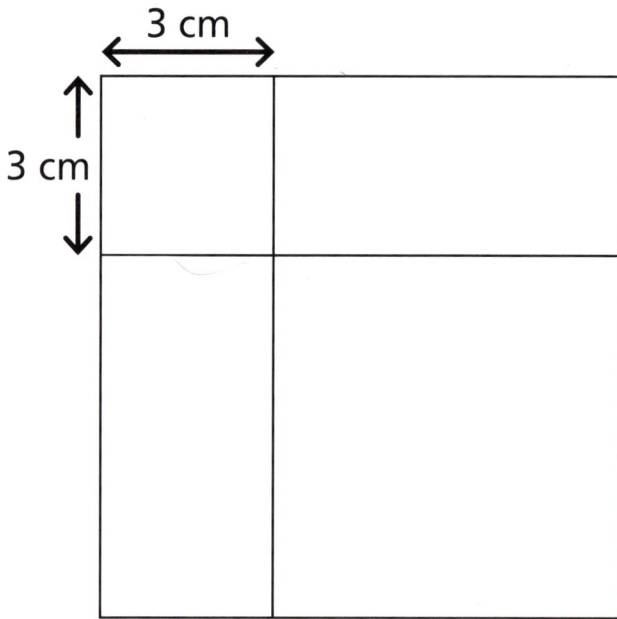

3 cm

3 cm

> I could use this method to draw accurate squares of different sizes.

b) Cut along the lines and measure the length of each side.

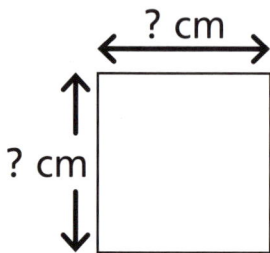

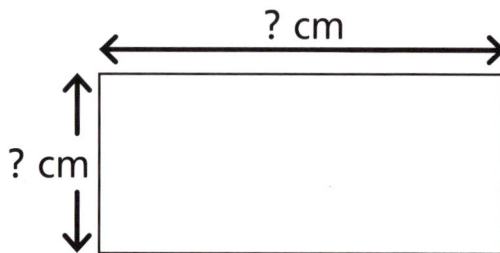

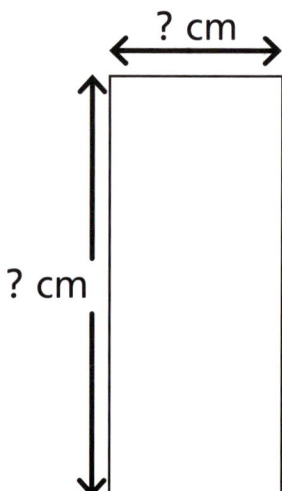

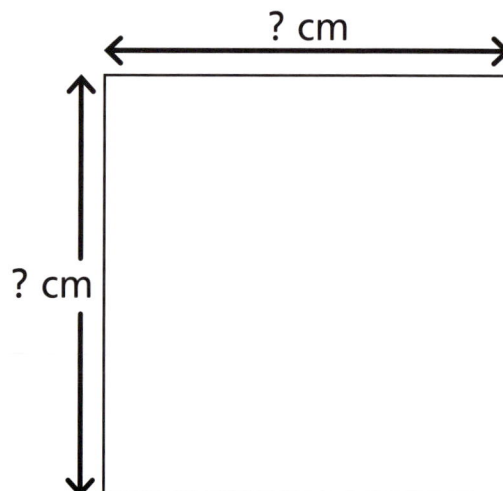

? cm

? cm

? cm

? cm

? cm

? cm

? cm

? cm

> I think I can predict the lengths, but I will measure to check how accurate I have been.

2 Draw these shapes using a ruler and a pencil.
Use squared paper to help you.

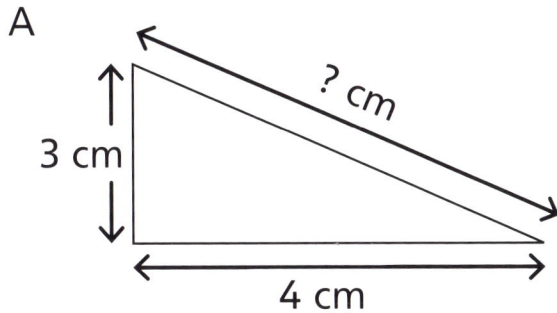

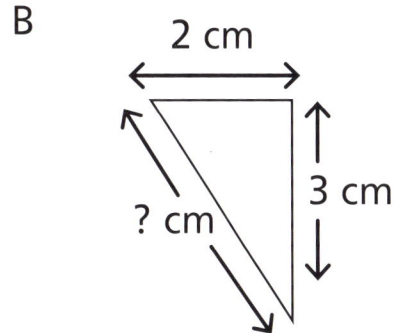

A

B

Measure the length of the third side of each triangle to the nearest millimetre.

3 Aki has a 3 cm square and a 7 cm square.

He draws lines joining opposite corners to make diagonal lines. Draw these squares and predict the length of the diagonal lines and then measure to check.

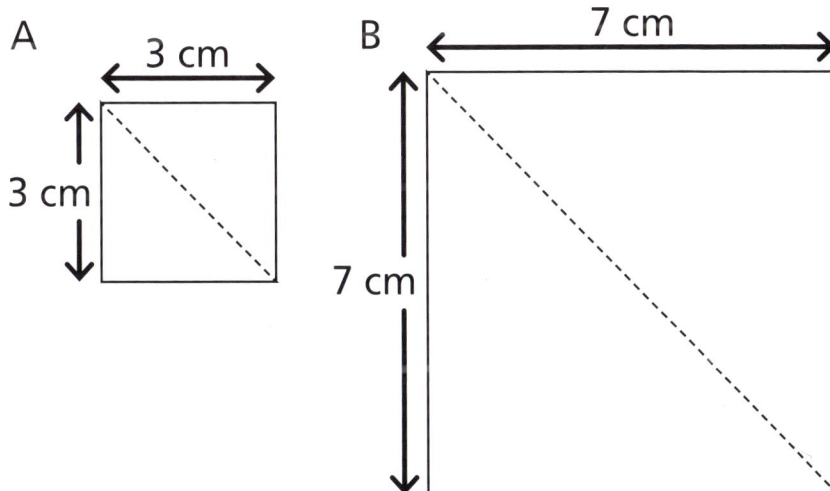

CHALLENGE

A

B

I will try to be accurate in my measurements by using centimetres and millimetres.

I predict the lines will be 3 cm and 7 cm long because all the sides of a square are the same length.

135

→ Practice book 3C p97

Horizontal and vertical

Discover

1 **a)** Explain why the books have fallen over on one shelf and not on the other.

b) How can the shelf be fixed?

Share

a)

I knew why! The shelf is not straight. One end is lower than the other end.

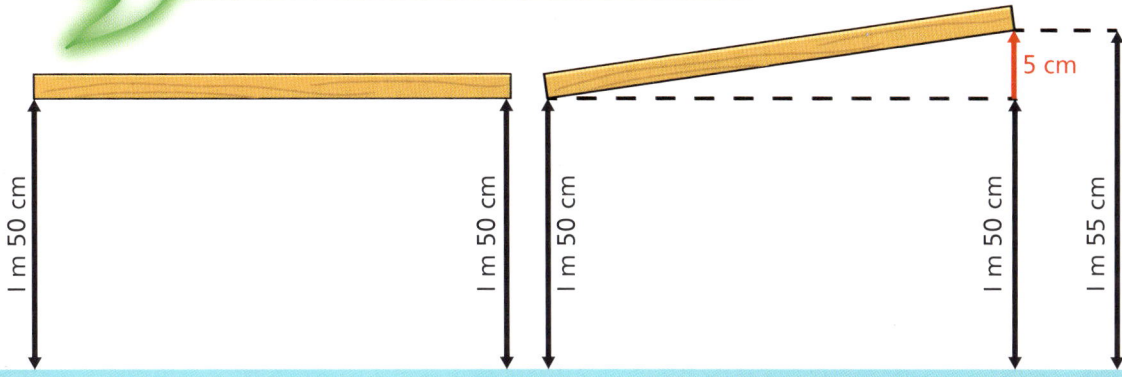

1 m 50 cm

1 m 50 cm

1 m 50 cm

5 cm

1 m 50 cm

1 m 55 cm

One shelf is horizontal. It is the same height all the way along.

One shelf is not horizontal. It is higher at one end than at the other end.

The word **horizontal** means a straight line that is perfectly level, from left to right.

The books stand upright on the horizontal shelf but have fallen over on the other shelf.

b) The shelf can be fixed by lowering the right-hand side to 1 m 50 cm.

I knew that the shelves should be 1 m 50 cm high.

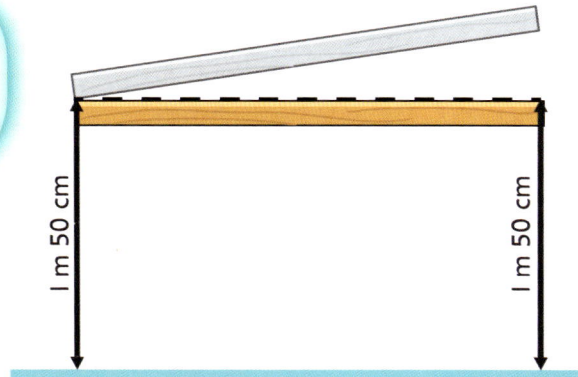

1 m 50 cm

1 m 50 cm

Think together

1 What is the same and what is different about these fences?

A 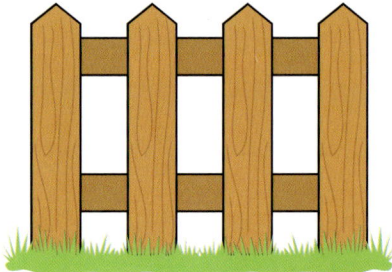   B 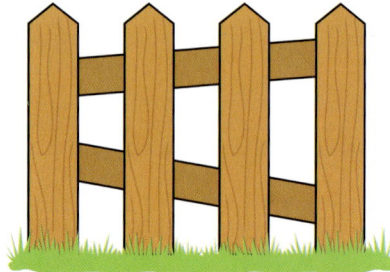   C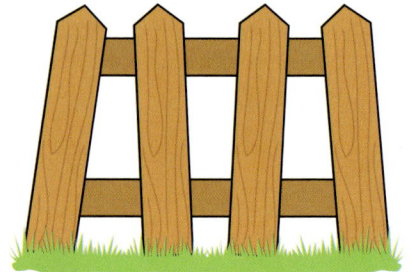

A **vertical** line forms a right angle with a horizontal line.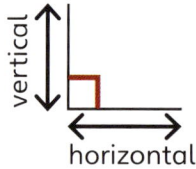

I wonder if I could use the words **horizontal** and **vertical** to answer the question.

2 You can use a plumb line to test if something is vertical. Find some vertical lines to test in your classroom.

A plumb line is a piece of string with a weight on the end. The weight keeps the string hanging straight down, or vertical.

3 **a)** Do any of these shapes have lines of symmetry?
If so, are the lines vertical, horizontal or both?

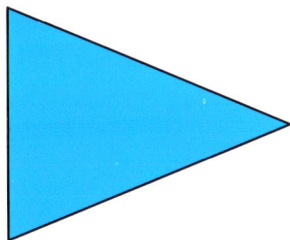

A

C

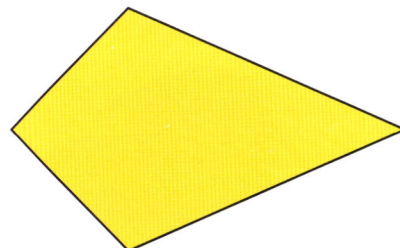

E

B

D

F

I remember that lines of symmetry can be vertical.

I think some of these have horizontal lines of symmetry.

b) Draw some shapes that each have a horizontal line of symmetry.

139

→ **Practice book 3C p100**

Parallel and perpendicular

Discover

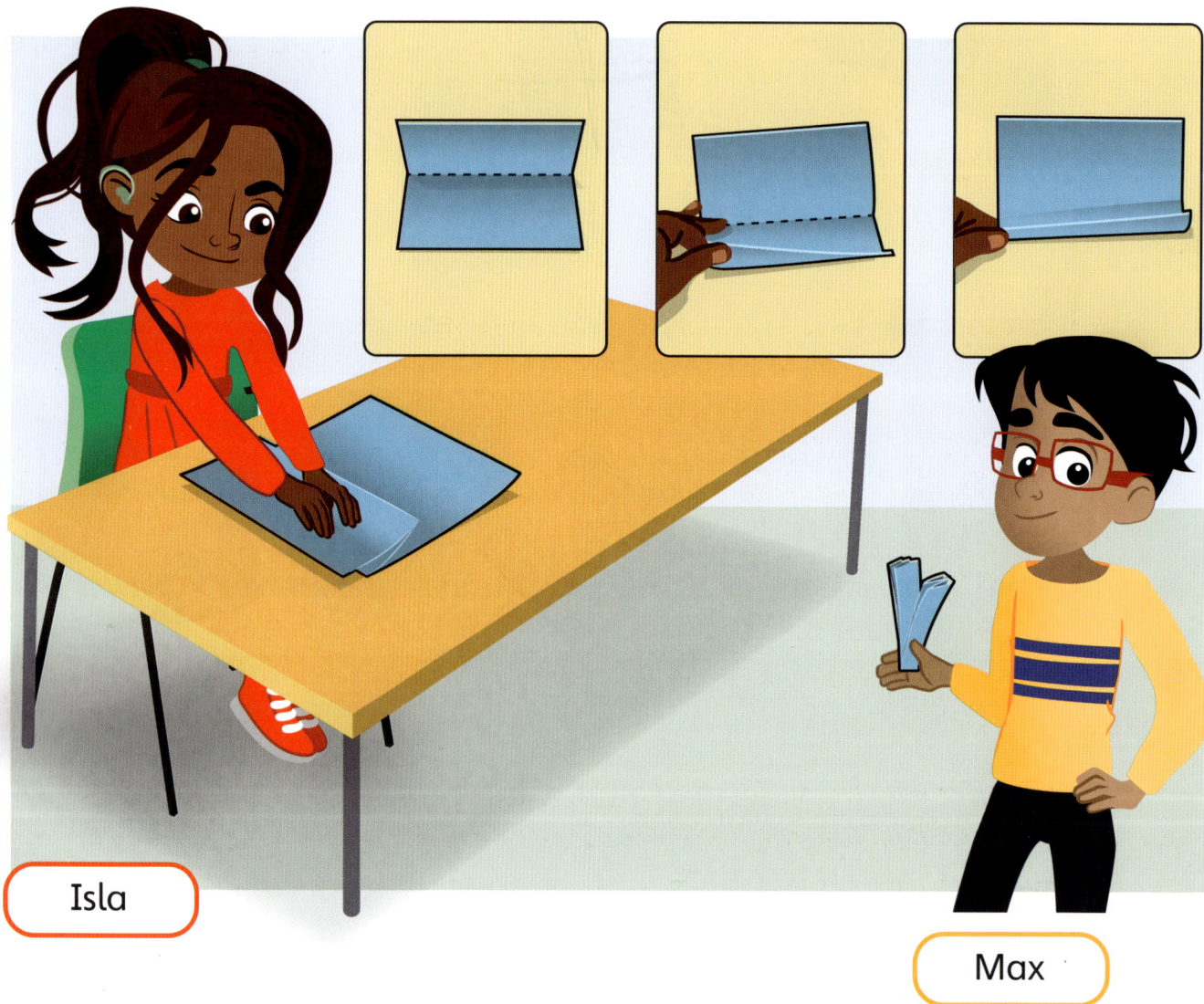

Isla

Max

1 **a)** Isla folds her paper into a concertina. What will it look like when she unfolds it?

b) Max folds his concertina in half. What will his look like when he unfolds it?

Share

a)

10cm   10cm   10cm   10cm

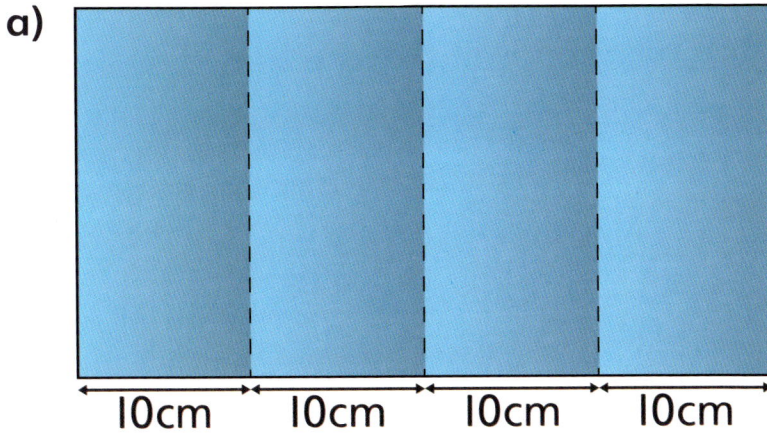

When Isla unfolds the paper, she will see parallel lines made by the folds.

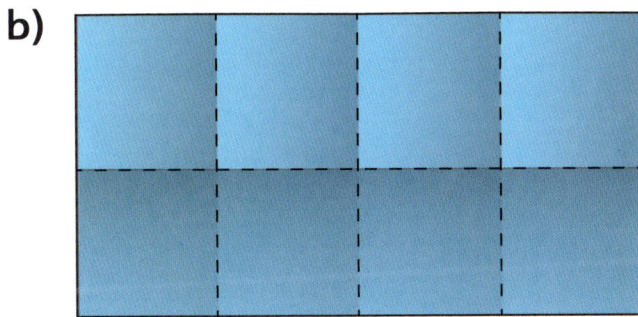

Lines that stay the same distance apart are called **parallel** lines. Lines that meet at a right angle are **perpendicular**.

b)

When Max unfolds his paper, it will have parallel lines like Isla's, but also perpendicular lines where he has folded his paper in half.

I wonder if two parallel lines will ever cross over each other.

Even if you had parallel lines 100 or a 1,000 miles long, they would still never touch.

Think together

1   Find the parallel and perpendicular lines in this picture.

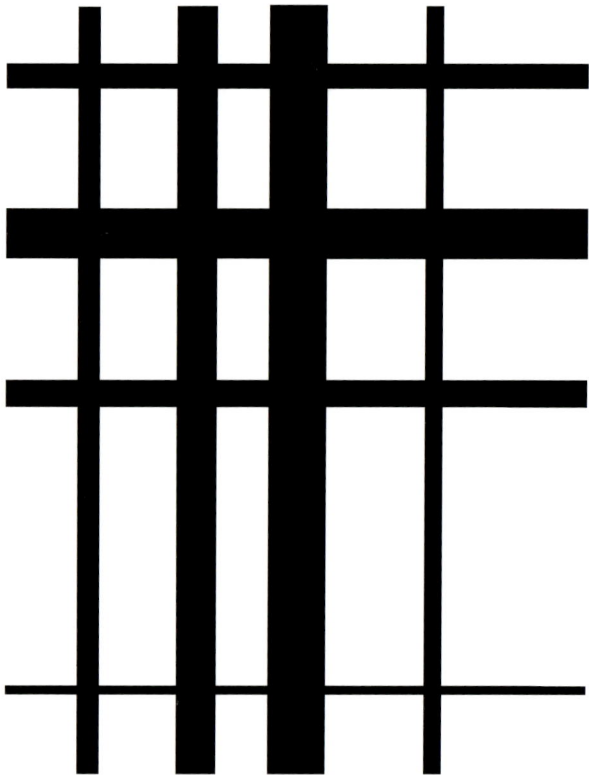

Perpendicular lines are at right angles to each other.

I can see both horizontal and vertical parallel lines.

2   Create your own parallel lines by drawing along both sides of a ruler. Why does this create parallel lines?

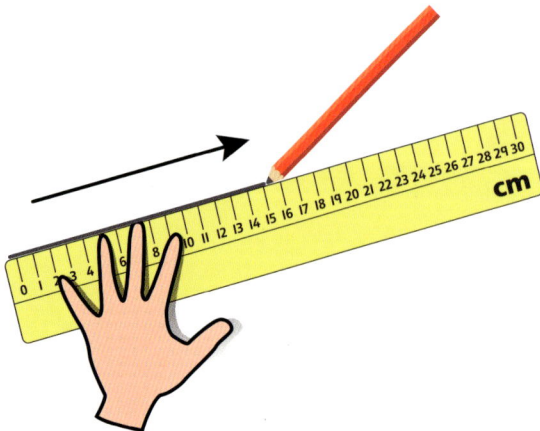

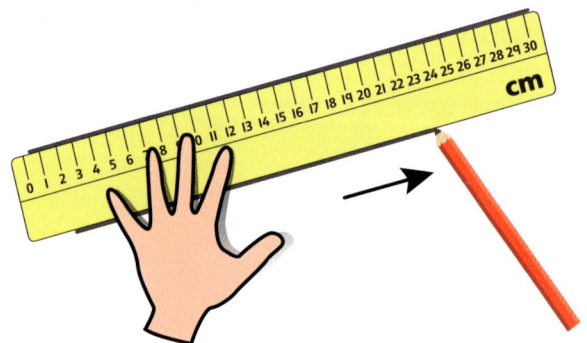

3 **a)** Look at these pairs of lines. Emma says they are all parallel because they do not cross over. Explain whether you agree or not.

A   B   C   D

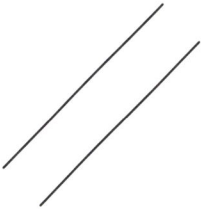   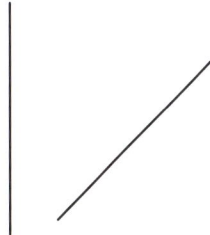   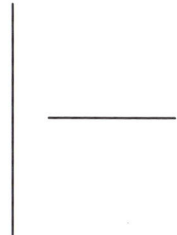

> None of these pairs of lines cross over, but I am not sure if they are all parallel.

b) How could you draw lines parallel to each of these?

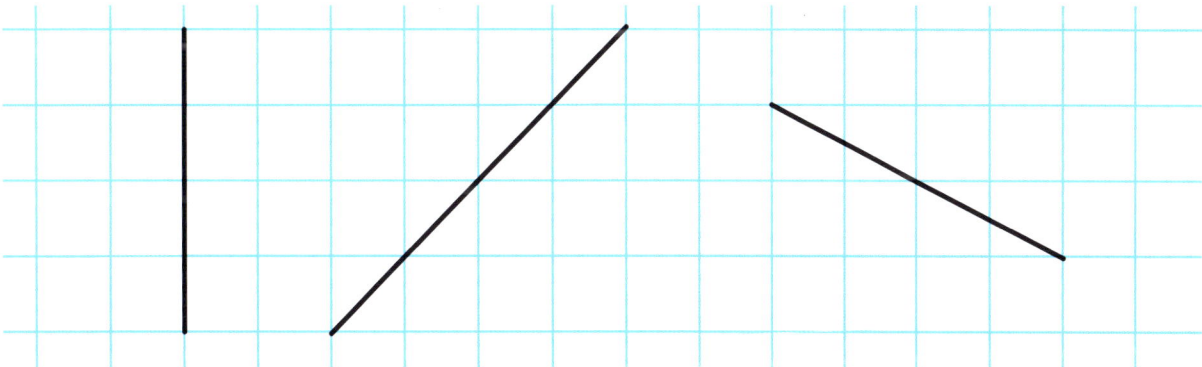

> I can draw more than two lines parallel to the vertical line.

143

→ **Practice book 3C p103**

Recognise, draw and describe 2D shapes

Discover

Make a quadrilateral.

1 **a)** What type of quadrilateral have the children made?

How many pairs of parallel lines does this shape have?

b) Would this shape have a different number of parallel lines if it were another size?

Share

a)

I used sticks to make the shape.

A quadrilateral is the name for any shape that has four sides.

There are two pairs of parallel lines in this shape.

The children have made a rectangle.
It has two pairs of parallel sides.

b) All rectangles, including squares, have two pairs of parallel lines.

Opposite sides of a rectangle are the same length. The lines joining them must be parallel.

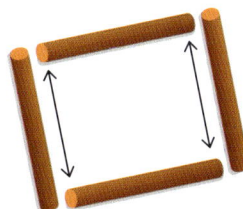

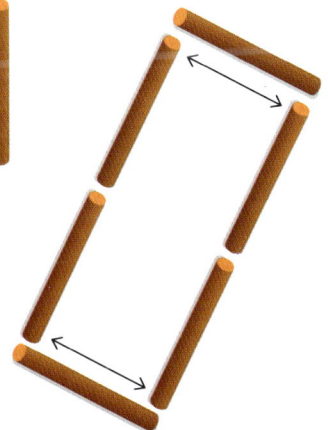

Think together

1 Which of these shapes have right angles?

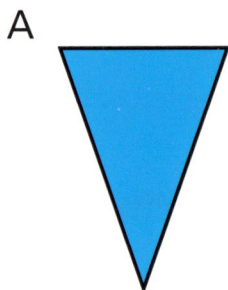

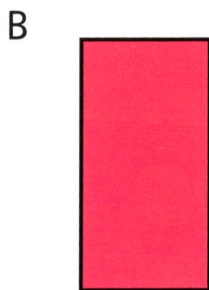

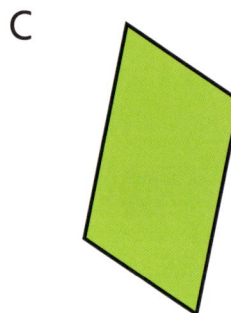

A   B   C

2 Here are four shapes.

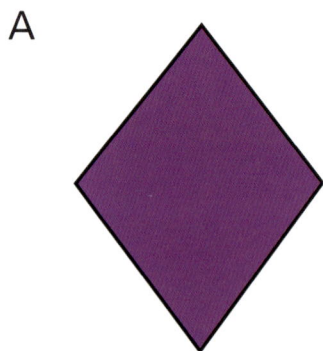

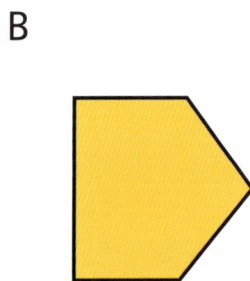

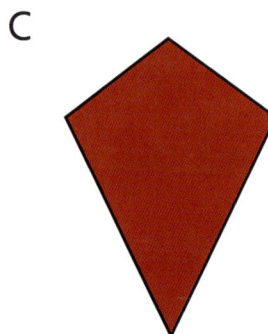

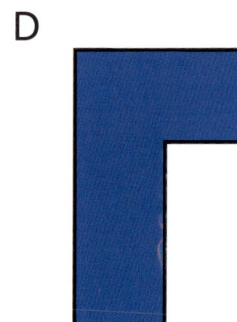

A   B   C   D

a) Which shapes are quadrilaterals?

b) Which shape is a hexagon?

c) Can you find a pentagon?

d) Which shapes have parallel sides?

e) Which shapes have perpendicular sides?

CHALLENGE

3 Complete Dexter's shape on your own piece of squared paper.

> I drew dots for each corner of my shape. I will use a ruler to join the dots.

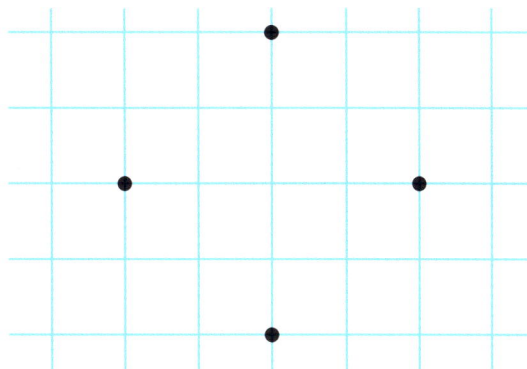

Use squared or dotted paper to draw different 2D shapes.

Talk about the features of your shapes using these words:

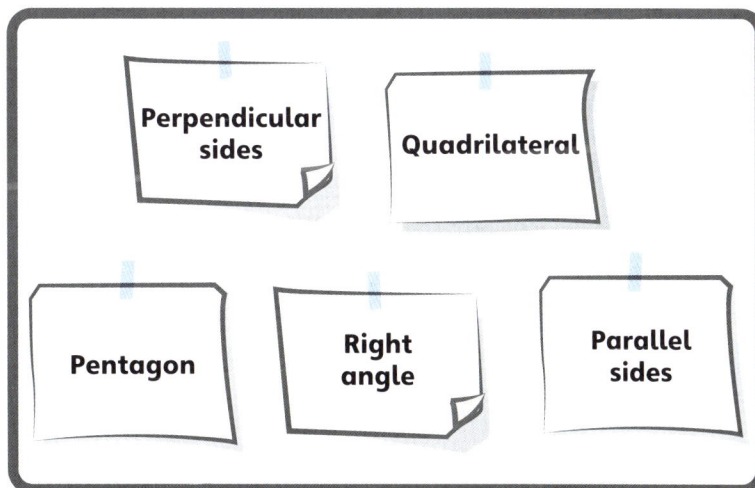

Perpendicular sides

Quadrilateral

Pentagon

Right angle

Parallel sides

147

→ Practice book 3C p106

Recognise and describe 3D shapes

Discover

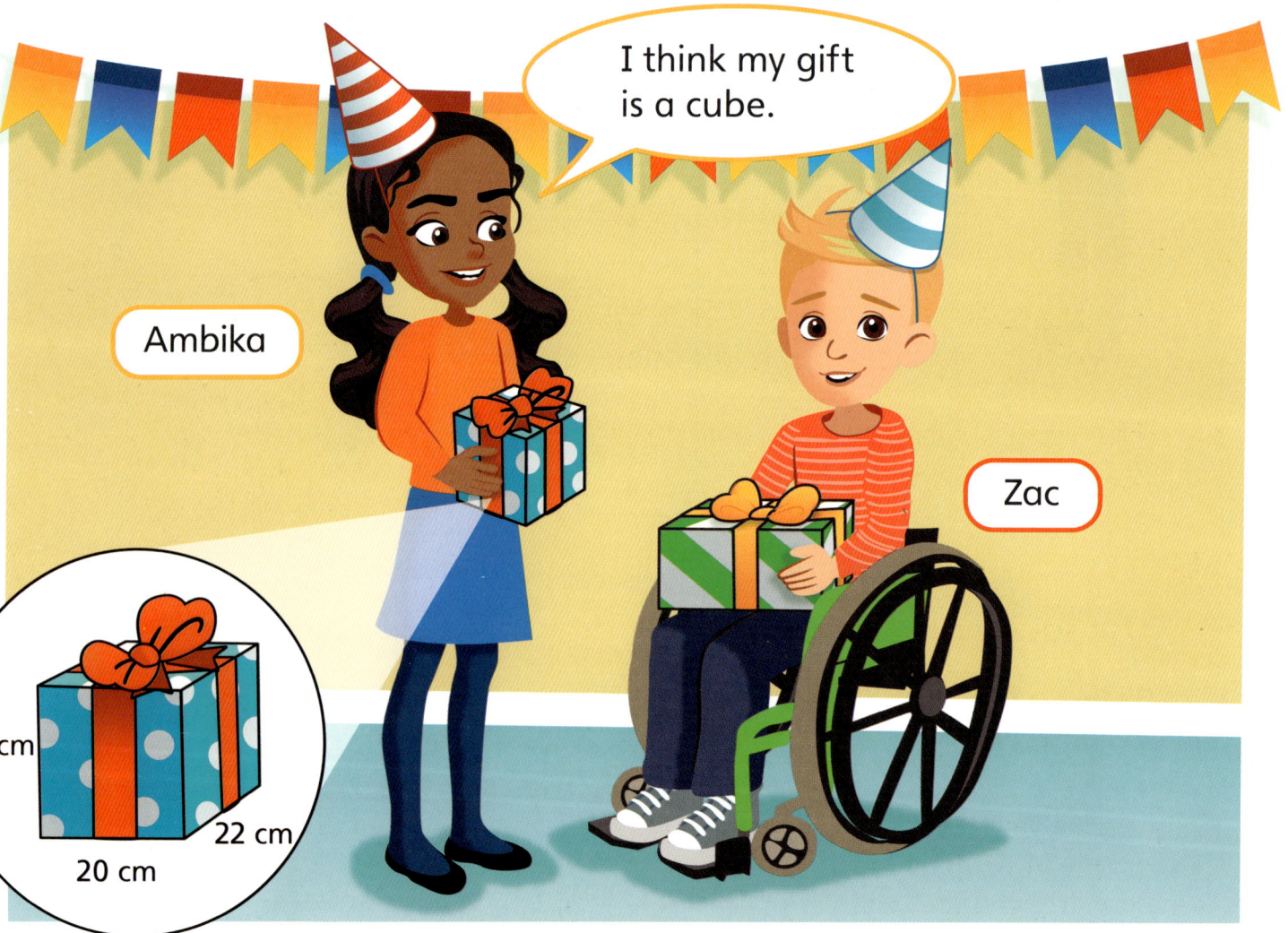

I think my gift is a cube.

Ambika

Zac

25 cm
22 cm
20 cm

① **a)** How can Ambika find out if her gift is a cube?

b) Ambika then measures the faces of her gift. Is it a cube?

Share

a) A cube is a special type of cuboid where all the edges are the same length, and each face is a square.

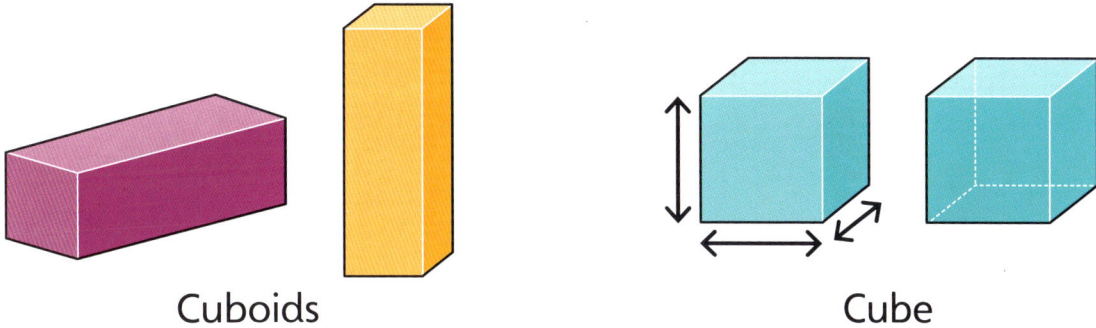

Cuboids   Cube

Ambika can measure all the edges of her gift to find out if it is a cube.

The edges are not all the same so Ambika's gift is not a cube.

25 cm
22 cm
20 cm

b)

I checked the angles to make sure that each face is a rectangle.

| Top / Bottom | Side / Side | Front / Back |

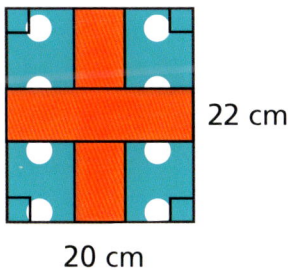
22 cm
20 cm

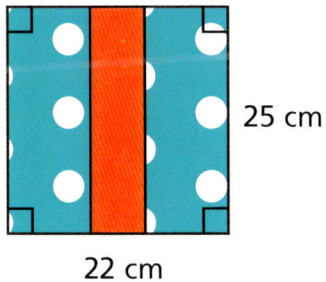
25 cm
22 cm

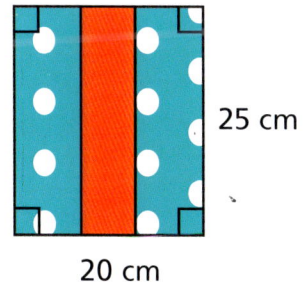
25 cm
20 cm

All the faces of Ambika's gift are rectangles. The opposite faces are exactly the same shape and size. Ambika's gift is a cuboid. It is not a cube because the faces are not squares.

149

Think together

1. Describe the faces of Zac's gift. How long are the edges of each one?

12 cm

12 cm

24 cm

> I thought only cubes had square faces, but cuboids can have them too.

2. What is the shape of this tent? Count the number of faces, vertices and edges.

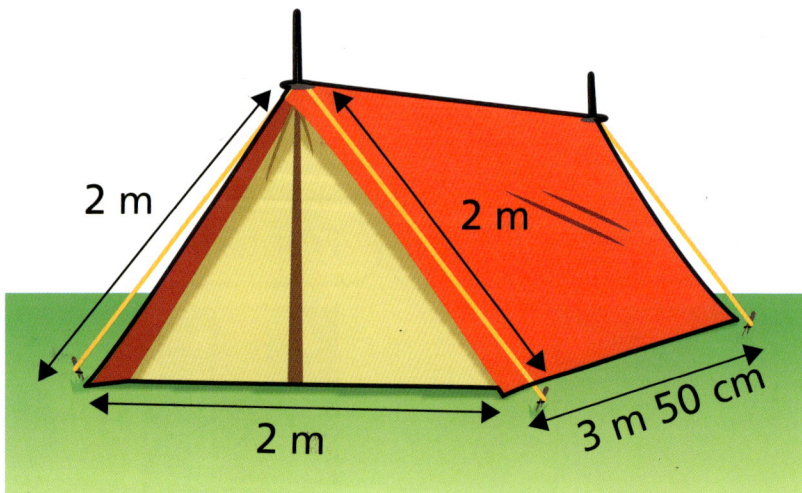

2 m

2 m

2 m

3 m 50 cm

> I can describe the measurements of each face.

CHALLENGE

3 Sort these shapes using the sorting circles.

If a shape does not fit into the circles, it must go outside the circles but inside the rectangle.

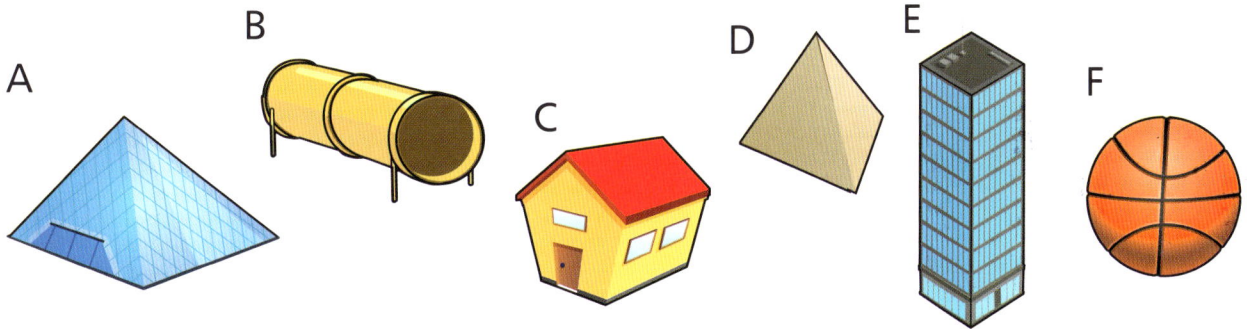

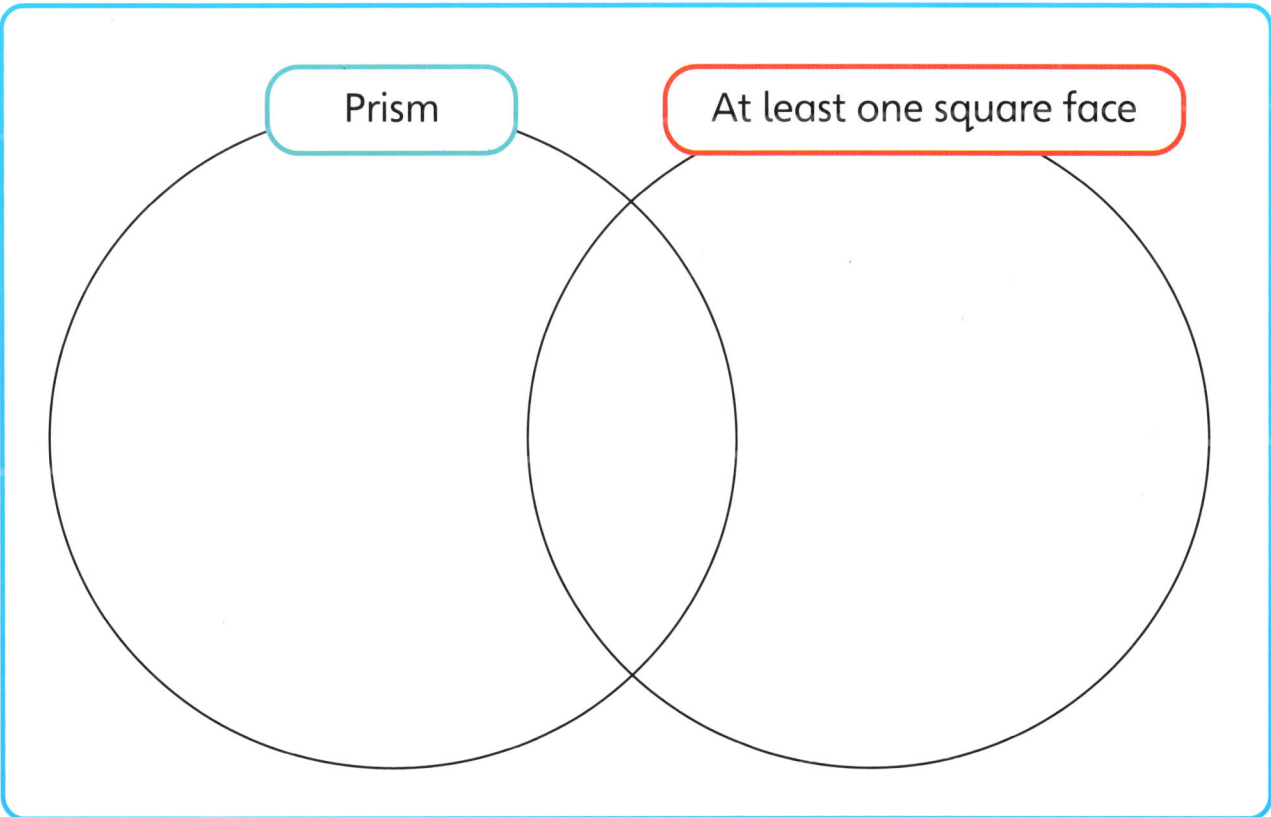

A   B   C   D   E   F

Prism   At least one square face

→ **Practice book 3C p109**

Make 3D shapes

Discover

Lee

Bella

1 a) Lee and Bella both want to make a large cube. Who can make a large cube using all of their smaller cubes?

b) Lee thinks he can make five different cuboids using all of his small cubes. Is he correct?

Share

a)

Bella's

Lee's

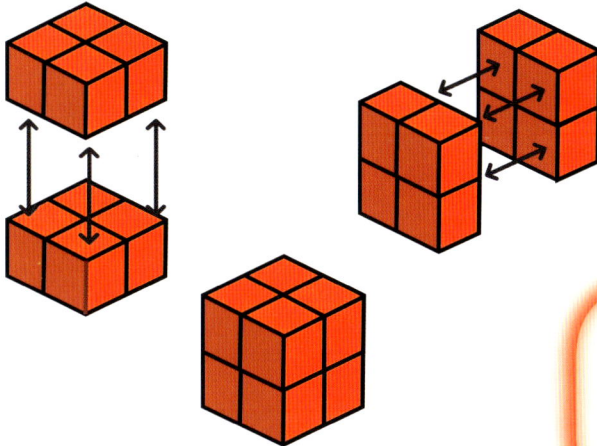

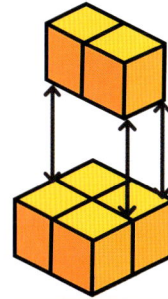

Lee does not have enough small cubes to make a large cube.

Bella can make a cube by using all of her smaller cubes. It has a length of 2 units in every direction.

b)

Cuboid 1

Cuboid 2

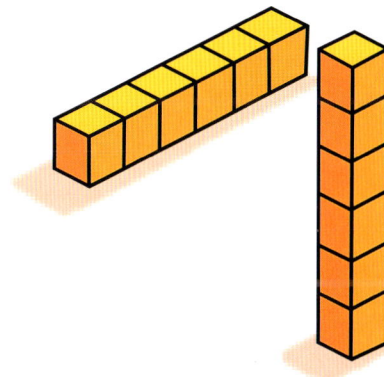

Lee is not correct: he can only make two different cuboids.

He might think he can make five because he can show them from different angles by placing different faces on the table.

Think together

1 Make some cubes using different construction materials.
How many of each will you need?

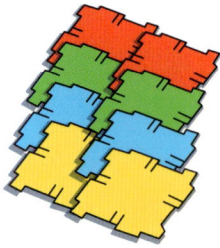

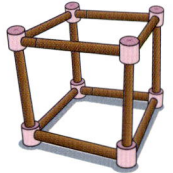

You need ☐ squares to make the faces of a cube.

You need ☐ sticks to make the edges of a cube.

You need ☐ marshmallows to make the corners (vertices) of a cube.

2 Some children want to make a cube, a sphere, and a pyramid.

a) Which of the shapes can they make from each set of materials?

b) Which shape cannot be made from any of these materials?
Why is this?

sticks and
marshmallows

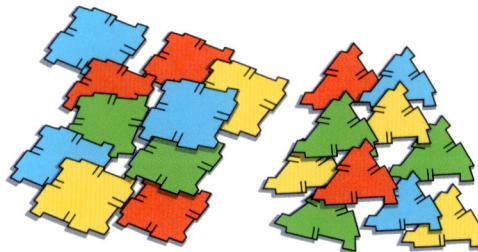

squares and
triangles

linking cubes

CHALLENGE

3 a) Which sets of materials could be used to make these 3D shapes?

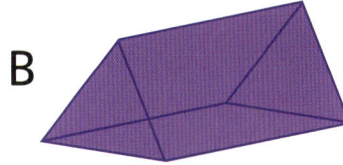

A

B

sticks and marshmallows

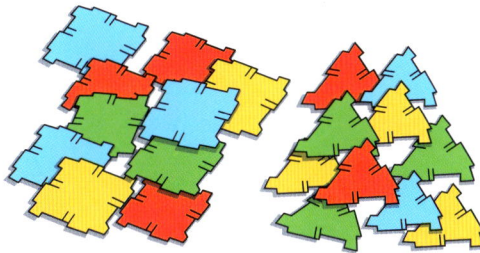

squares and triangles

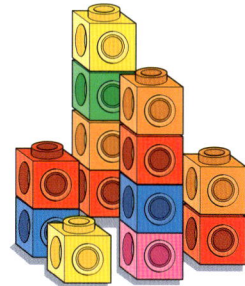

linking cubes

I will make a list of which materials can and cannot make each 3D shape.

I cannot use the cubes to make a circle face. I will need to think of a different material.

b) How many pieces of each material would you need to make the prism?

155

End of unit check

1 Which shape has just one right angle?

A

C

B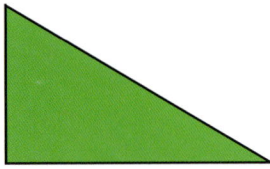

D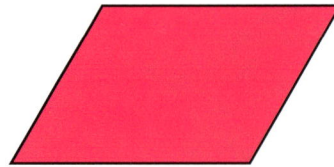

2 Which turn shows an obtuse angle?

A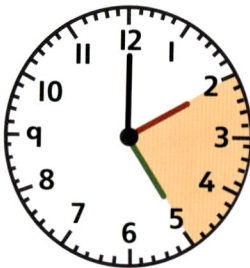

B

C

D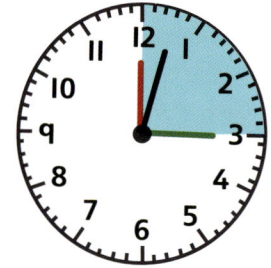

3 Which of these shows three horizontal lines?

A

B

C

D

4 Identify the shape with perpendicular lines.

A

C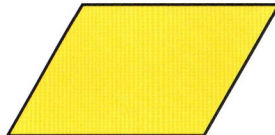

B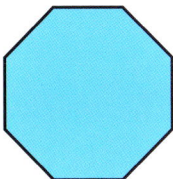

D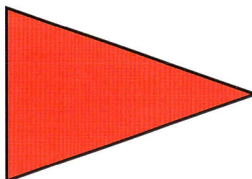

5 Identify the shape with no pairs of parallel lines.

A

C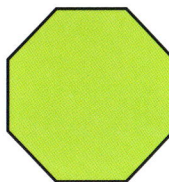

B

D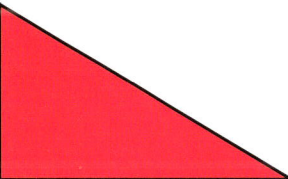

6 Sketch the faces of this shape on squared paper.
Include the measurements.

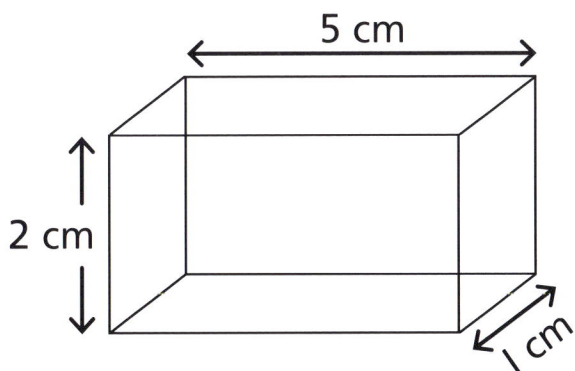

→ Practice book 3C p115

Unit 15
Statistics

In this unit we will …

⚡ Present information in different ways

⚡ Use pictograms, bar charts and tables

⚡ Answer questions based on information that is presented in different ways

This looks like the block diagrams we used last year. I wonder what it is called.

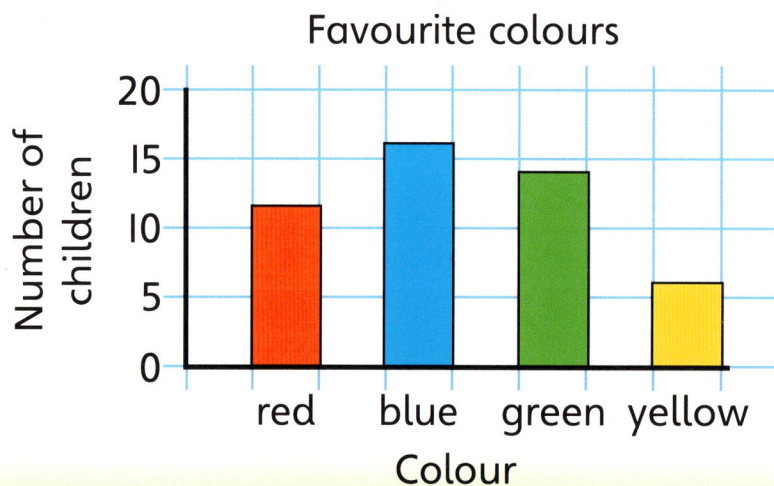

Favourite colours

Number of children

20
15
10
5
0

red   blue   green   yellow

Colour

We will need some maths words. Which ones have you seen before?

pictogram   key   bar chart

scale   table   row

column   vertical axis

We need pictograms too! Work out how many people like skiing.

Sport	Number of people
skiing	☺ ☺ ☺ ☺ ☺
snowboarding	☺ ☺ ☺ ☺ ☺ ☺

Key: Each ☺ represents 2 people.

Interpret pictograms ❶

Discover

Mini-beasts	Number of mini-beasts
butterfly	🔵 🔵 🔵
beetle	🔵 🔵 🔵 🔵
spider	🔵 ◖

Key: Each 🔵 represents 2 mini-beasts.

Amelia

❶ Amelia searched in her garden for mini-beasts. She recorded her results in a pictogram.

a) How many beetles did Amelia find?

b) How many spiders did Amelia find?

Share

a) From the key we know that each symbol represents 2 mini-beasts.

beetle	🔵 🔵 🔵 🔵

I used a number line to check the answer.

There are 4 symbols for beetles.

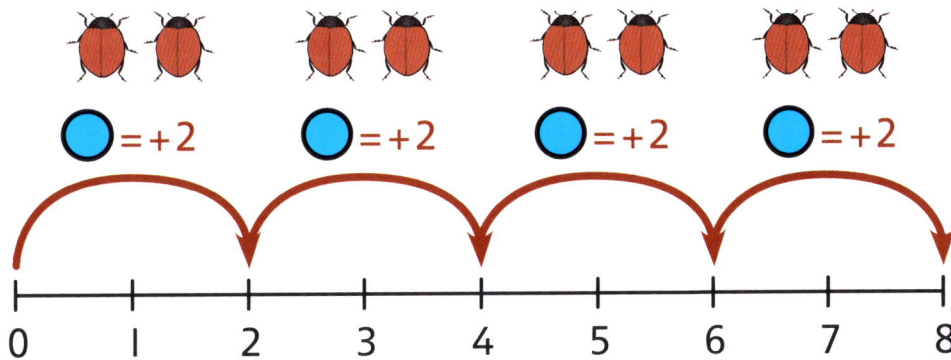

$$4 \times 2 = 8$$

$$2 + 2 + 2 + 2 = 8$$

Amelia found 8 beetles.

b) There are 1 and a half symbols for spiders.

spider	🔵 ◖

A whole symbol represents 2 spiders.

Half of 2 is 1.

So, ◖ represents 1 spider.

$$2 + 1 = 3$$

Amelia found 3 spiders.

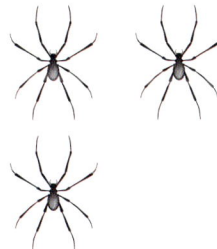

Think together

1. Amelia counted flowers in her garden.

   The pictogram shows her results.

Flowers	Number of flowers
bluebell	🌸 🌸
honeysuckle	🌸 🌸 🌸 🌸 🌸
daffodil	🌸 🌸 🌸
primrose	🌸

Key: Each 🌸 represents 10 flowers.

a) How many honeysuckles did Amelia find?

b) How many daffodils did Amelia find?

c) How do you know by looking at the pictogram that Amelia found more bluebells than primroses?

d) How many more bluebells than primroses did she find?

2 Amelia created this pictogram showing the different trees she found.

She found 15 birch trees.

a) How much is each symbol worth?

b) How many conifer trees did she find?

c) How many trees did she find in total?

Tree	Number of trees
birch	🌳 🌳 🌳
oak	🌳 🌳
conifer	🌳 🌳 🌳 🌳

Key: Each 🌳 represents ☐ trees.

CHALLENGE

3 Lee also searched for mini-beasts. He made this pictogram.

Mini-beasts	Number of mini-beasts
butterfly	🦋 🦋
beetle	🐞 🐞 🐞 🐞 🐞
spider	🕷 🕷 🕷 🕷

Each 🦋 represents 5 butterflies.

Each 🐞 represents 1 beetle.

Each 🕷 represents 2 spiders.

How could you improve the pictogram so you can compare the results more easily?

I am going to check if he found the most beetles.

➜ **Practice book 3C p118**

Interpret pictograms 2

Discover

Favourite position	Number of children
goalkeeper	⚽ ⚽
midfield	⚽ ⚽ ⚽ ⚽ ⚽ ⚽
defender	⚽ ⚽ ⚽ ⚽ ⚽ ⚽
forward	⚽ ⚽ ⚽
striker	⚽ ⚽ ⚽ ⚽

Key: Each ⚽ represents 2 children.

1 Some children voted for their favourite football position.

a) How many more children chose midfield than goalkeeper?

b) How many children chose defender or forward as their favourite position?

Share

Each symbol represents the same number of children. I worked out the difference in the number of symbols first.

a)

goalkeeper	⚽ ⚽
midfield	⚽ ⚽ ⚽ ⚽ ⚽ ⚽

There are 4 more ⚽ symbols for midfield. Each symbol represents 2 children.

Astrid's method: There are 4 more balls in the row for midfield than in the row for goalkeeper. $4 \times 2 = 8$

Dexter's method: There are 2 balls in the row for goalkeeper and 6 balls in the row for midfield. $2 \times 2 = 4$ and $6 \times 2 = 12$

4 children chose goalkeeper and 12 chose midfield. $12 - 4 = 8$

So, 8 more children chose midfield than goalkeeper.

I did it a different way. I worked out how many children like each position first.

b)

defender	⚽ ⚽ ⚽ ⚽ ⚽ ◖
forward	⚽ ⚽ ◖

Method 1: For defender and forward there are 7 whole symbols and 2 half symbols altogether.

7 add 2 halves makes 8.

Each symbol represents 2 children. $8 \times 2 = 16$

Method 2: Look at the amounts separately. $11 + 5 = 16$

⚽ =   ◖ =

$5 \times 2 = 10$ $2 \times 2 = 4$

⚽ ⚽ ⚽ ⚽ ⚽ ◖   ⚽ ⚽ ◖

$10 + 1 = 11$ $4 + 1 = 5$

16 children chose defender or forward as their favourite position.

Think together

1 The pictogram shows the age of children in Raven Football Club.

Age of children in Raven Football Club	
Age	**Number of children**
age six	⚽ ⚽
age seven	⚽ ⚽ ⚽ ⚽
age eight	⚽ ⚽ ⚽ ⚽ ⚽ ⚽
age nine	⚽ ⚽ ⚽ ⚽
age ten	⚽ ⚽ ⚽ ⚽ ⚽

Key: Each ⚽ represents 2 children.

a) How many more seven-year-olds are there than six-year-olds?

b) How many seven- and eight-year-olds are there altogether?

c) How many players are in Raven Football Club altogether?

> I think there are two different ways I could work this out. I think one might be quicker.

> I wonder if I need to work out each row separately.

2 This pictogram shows the number of goals scored by the four top-scoring players.

How many more goals has the top goal scorer scored compared to the next highest goal scorer?

Name	Number of goals
Jamilla	🏆🏆🏆🏆🏆
Lee	🏆🏆
Luis	🏆🏆🏆
Olivia	🏆🏆

Key: Each 🏆 represents 10 goals.

3 This pictogram shows the number of games played by 44 children in Heron FC. Some information is missing.

CHALLENGE

a) How many children have played 5 or more games for Heron FC this season?

b) How many children have played 3 games?

Number of games	Number of children
3 games	
4 games	⚽⚽⚽⚽⚽
5 games	⚽⚽⚽◖
6 games	⚽⚽⚽⚽◖
7 games	⚽⚽⚽◖

Key: Each ⚽ represents 2 children.

You can use your answer from part a) to help you with part b).

→ Practice book 3C p121

Draw pictograms

Discover

Let's make a pictogram to represent our data.

Miss Hall

How children travel to school		
Method	Tally	Number
walk |卌 卌 ||	12
car	卌	4
bike	卌 ||||	9
bus	||	2

1 **a)** Miss Hall has made a mistake. One of the numbers is incorrect. Which one?

b) Draw a pictogram to represent the data in the tally chart.

Draw a circle to represent 1 child.

Share

a) The tally marks show the number of children who travel to school by each method of transport.

There are five tallies for travelling by car.

Miss Hall has said the number of children is 4.

It should be 5.

b)

How children travel to school		
Method	**Tally**	**Number**
walk	⬤⬤⬤⬤⬤⬤⬤⬤⬤⬤⬤⬤	12
car	⬤⬤⬤⬤⬤	5
bike	⬤⬤⬤⬤⬤⬤⬤⬤⬤	9
bus	⬤⬤	2

Key: Each ⬤ represents 1 child

> I used some circle stickers instead of drawing the circles.

Think together

1. Some children were asked what type of pets they have.

What pets children have		
Type of pet	Tally	Number
dog	卌 卌 ||||	14
cat	||||	4
rabbit	|||	3
other	卌	5
none	卌 卌	10

a) There are 28 children in the class.

Explain why the tally chart might not total to 28.

b) Miss Hall wants the class to use a symbol to represent 2 children instead of 1.

Why might she want to do this?

c) Which of these symbols could be used?

Which symbols would you not use?

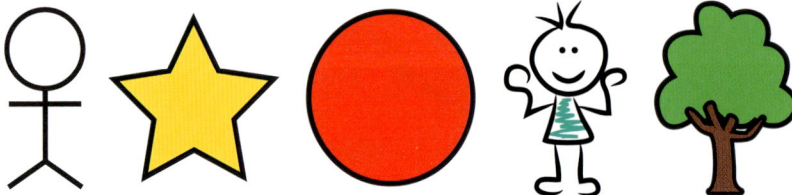

d) Make the pictogram for the data in the table using a symbol to represent 2 children.

2 Here is some data about the number of children in four classes.

Draw a circle to represent 4 children.

Class	Number of children in class
3A	28
4A	30
5A	25
6A	18

a) Draw a pictogram to represent this data.

b) Why might it not be a good idea to draw a circle to represent 5 children?

CHALLENGE

3 What mistakes has Emma made in drawing this pictogram?

Favourite flavour of ice cream	
chocolate	🍦🍦🍦
strawberry	🍦🍦🍦🍦🍦
vanilla	🔵🔵
other	🍦🍦🍦🍦🍦

Key: Each 🍦 represents 2 children.

→ **Practice book 3C p124**

Interpret bar charts ❶

Discover

Creatures we found in the rock pool

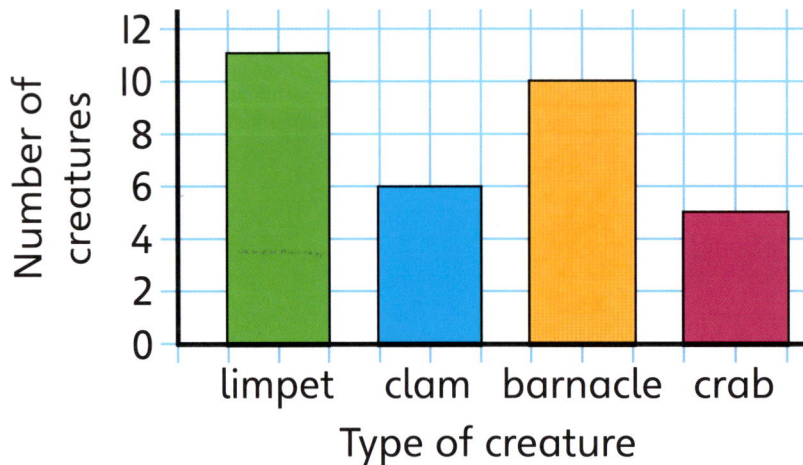

❶ **a)** How many clams and barnacles did the children find?

b) How many limpets did the children find?

Share

a) This is a **bar chart**. Use the scale on the vertical axis to find the value of each bar.

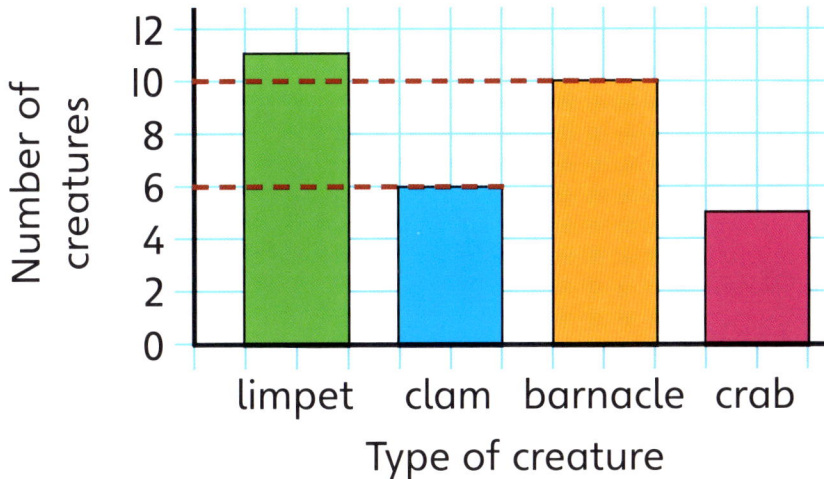

The line that goes up the side of the bar chart is called the **vertical axis**. The numbers are called the scale.

The children found 6 clams and 10 barnacles.

The children found 16 clams and barnacles altogether.

Use a ruler to draw a line from the vertical axis to the top of the bar you are looking at.

b) The height of the bar for limpets is half-way between 10 and 12 on the vertical axis.

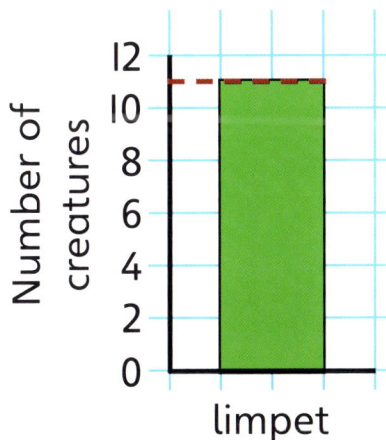

I read the scale like a number line.

The children found 11 limpets.

Think together

1 The bar chart shows the number of plants found at a rock pool.

   a) How many gutweeds did the children find?

   b) How many sea lettuces did they find?

   c) How many pieces of coral weed and how many sea oaks did they find altogether?

Plants we found in the rock pool

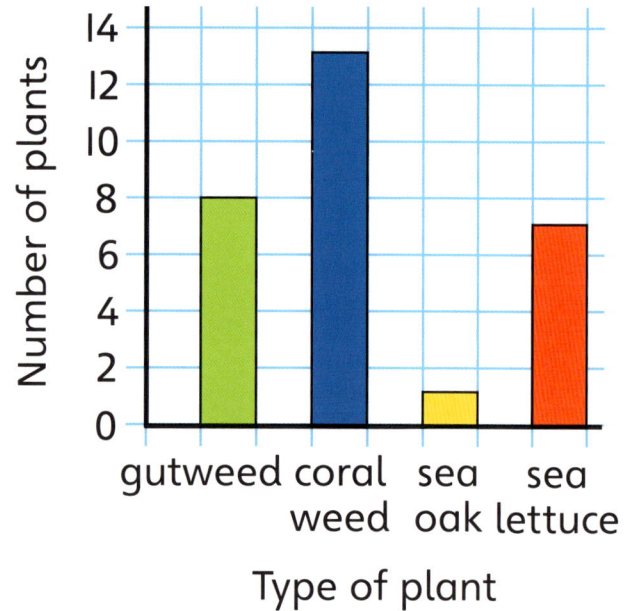

2 The bar chart shows the number of sea shells three children found.

   a) Who found the most shells?

   b) Who found the fewest shells?

   c) How many shells did each child find?

Results of the shell hunt

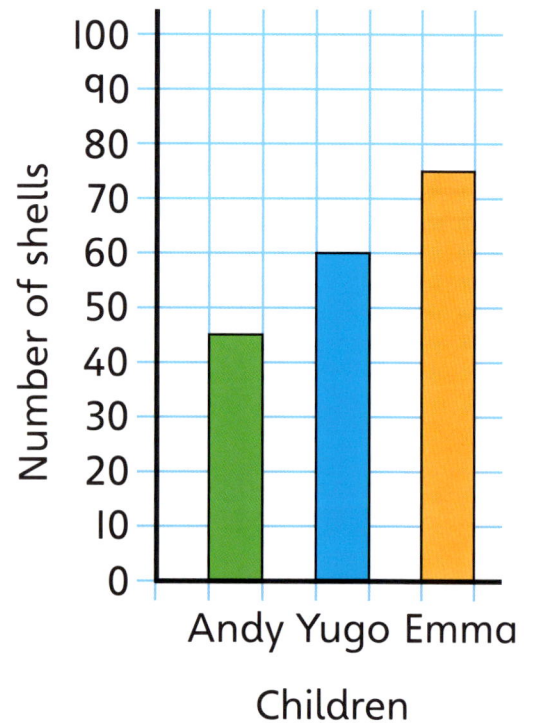

The scale goes up in 10s. I am going to work out what number is half-way between each 10.

3 Class 3A were asked to vote for their favourite sea animals.

Here are their votes.

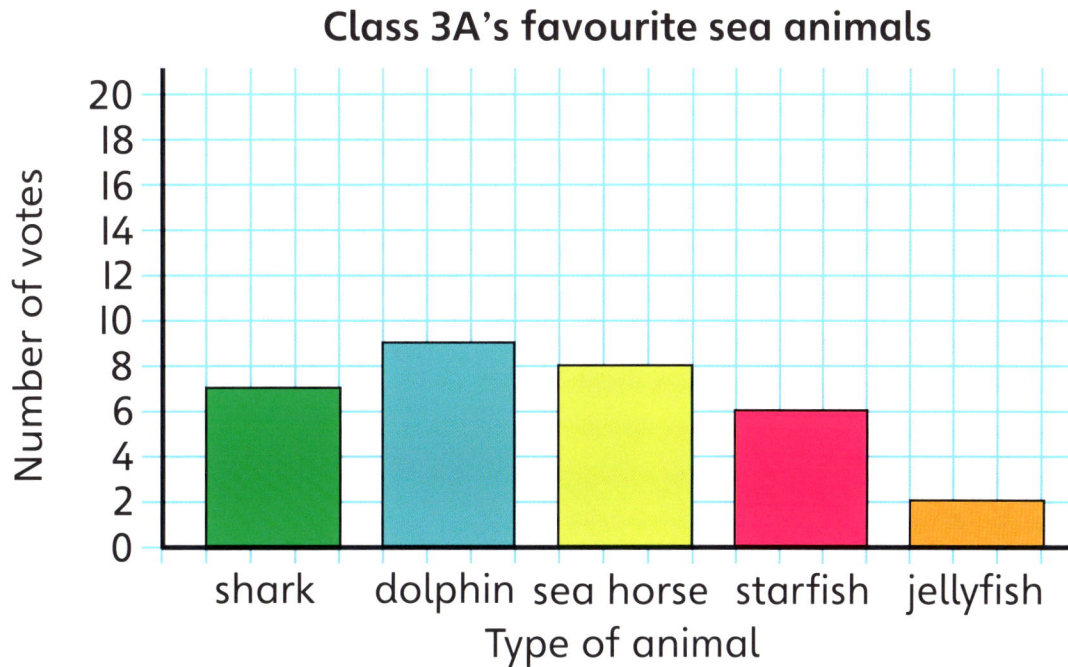

Class 3A's favourite sea animals

Write a short news summary for the school's magazine about the data.

I am going to mention which creatures are the most and least popular and think about why that might be the case.

I am going to mention how many children are in the class altogether.

175

→ **Practice book 3C p127**

Interpret bar charts 2

Discover

Holly Wood Academy Film Club

Favourite types of film at Holly Wood Academy

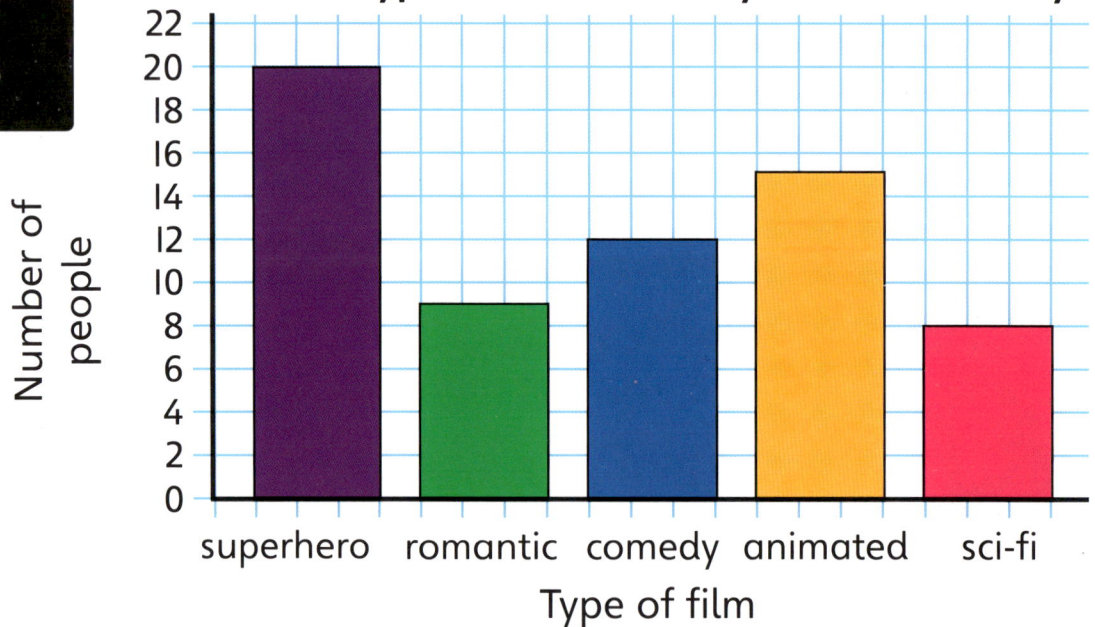

Number of people (y-axis): 0, 2, 4, 6, 8, 10, 12, 14, 16, 18, 20, 22

Type of film (x-axis): superhero, romantic, comedy, animated, sci-fi

1 a) How many more people like superhero films than like comedy films?

b) How many people like comedy or animated films best?

Share

a) You can draw lines, using a ruler, to read off the number of people.

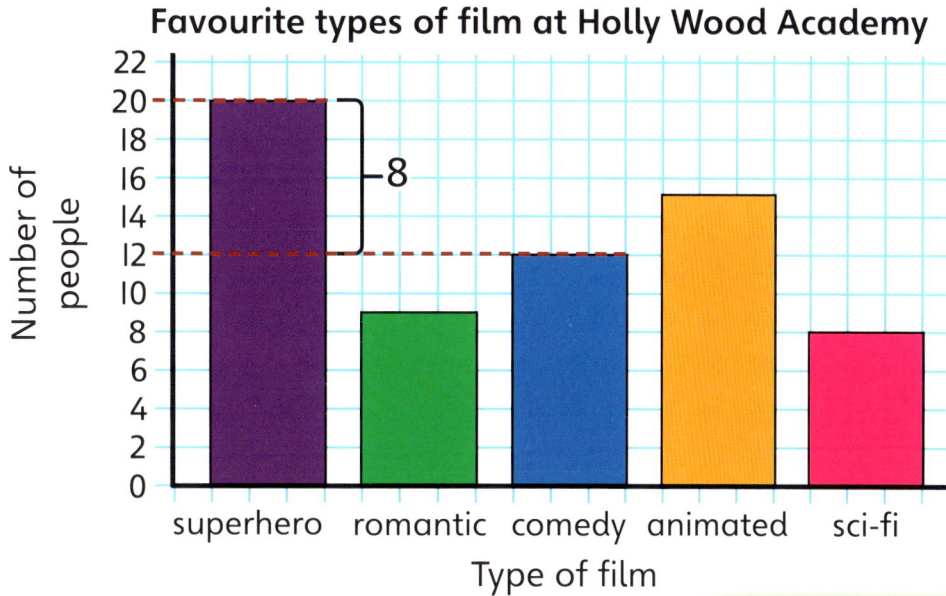

Favourite types of film at Holly Wood Academy

20 people like superhero films best.

12 people like comedy films best.

$20 - 12 = 8$

8 more people like superhero films than like comedy films.

> I read the values off the chart and found the difference.

b) 12 people like comedy films best.

15 people like animated films best.

$15 + 12 = 27$

	T	O
	1	5
+	1	2
	2	7

> I worked out how many people liked comedy and animated films then added these numbers together.

27 people like comedy or animated films best.

Think together

1   **a)** How many more sandwiches were sold than nachos?

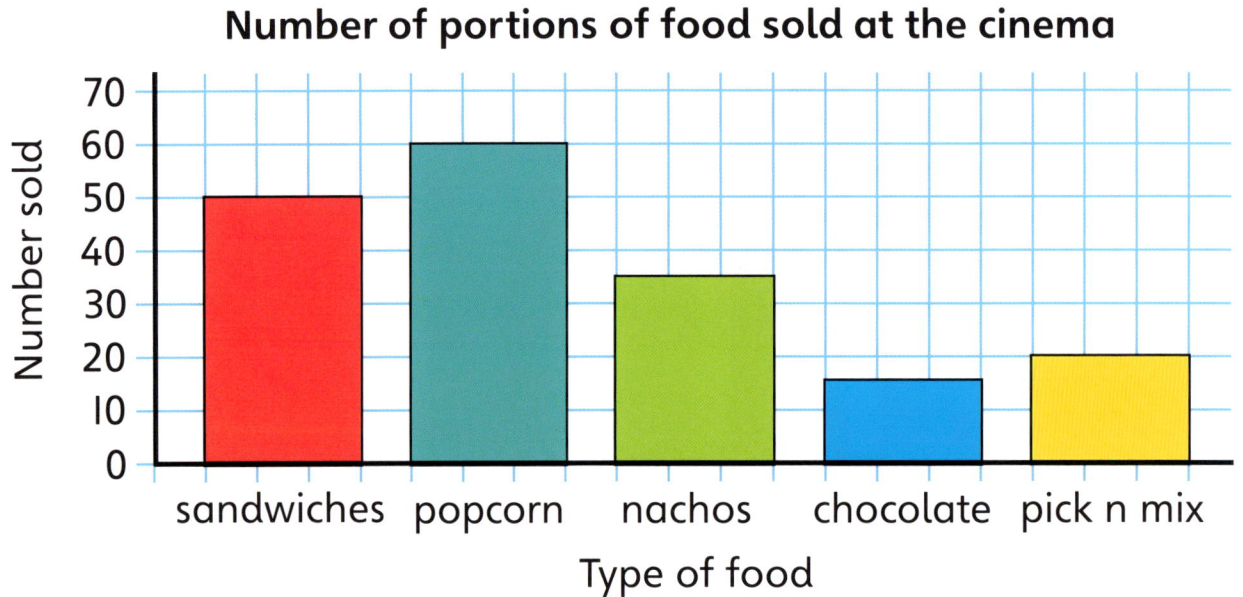

Number of portions of food sold at the cinema

b) Which were the most popular and least popular types of food?

Tell a partner how you know.

What is the difference in numbers sold between the most popular and the least popular food?

I am going to look at the tallest and shortest bars.

2 Class 3A drew a bar chart to represent the number of different tickets sold for a film.

Ticket type	Adult	Child	Student	Senior	Family
Number of people	20	25	40	15	20

Types of tickets sold for *Superheroes vs Turtles*

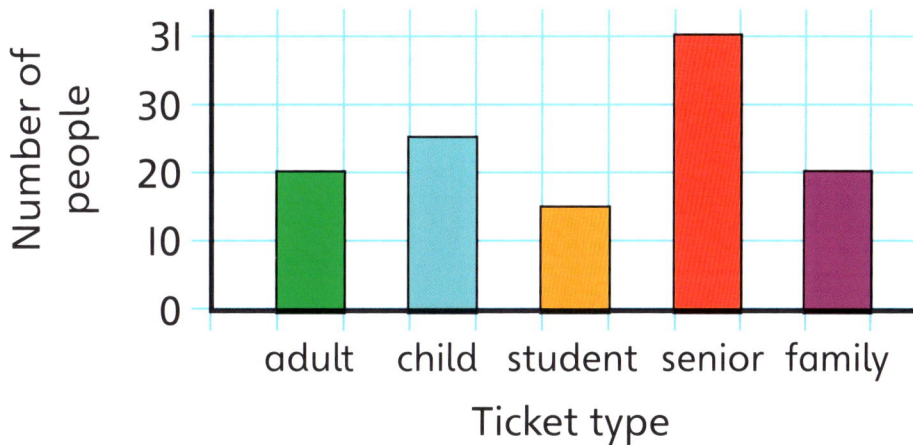

What mistakes did Class 3A make?

3 Do more people prefer to go to the cinema during the week or at the weekend?

CHALLENGE

Favourite day to go to the cinema

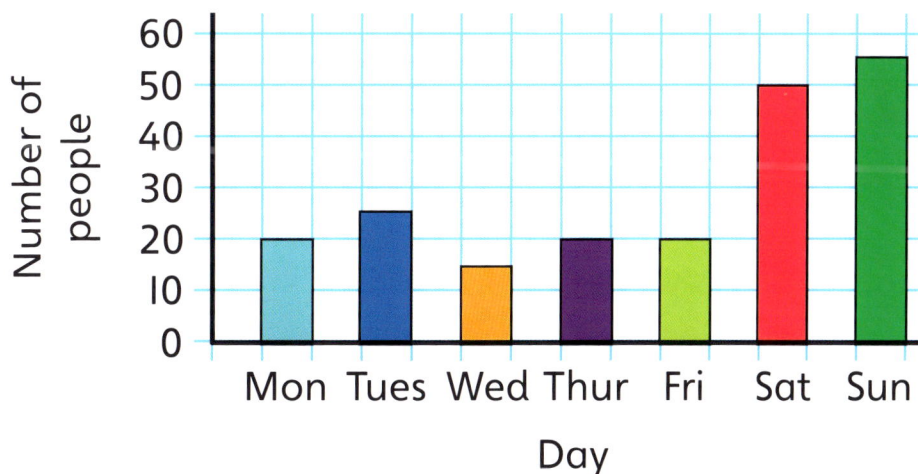

➜ **Practice book 3C p130**

Collect and represent data in a bar chart

Discover

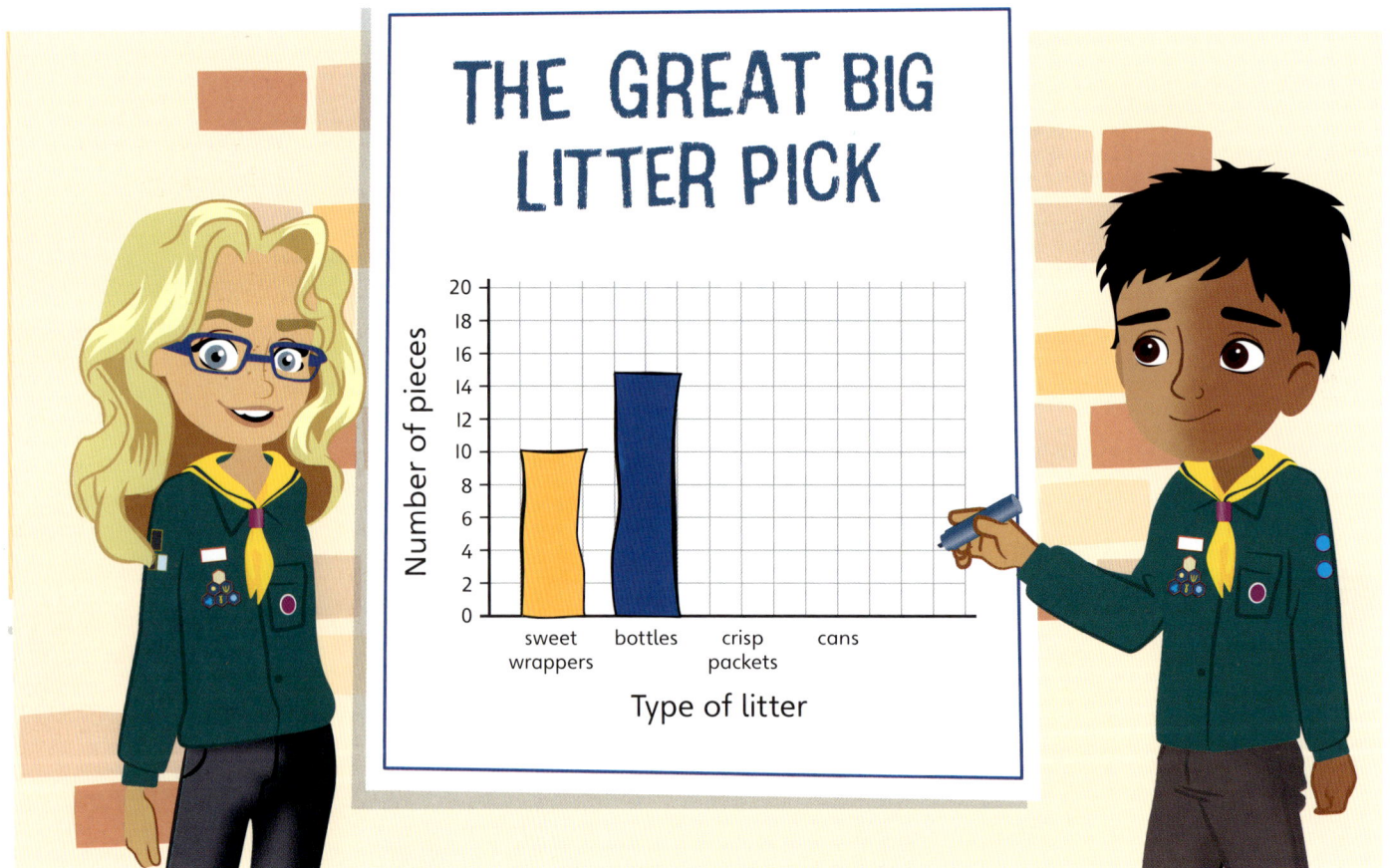

THE GREAT BIG LITTER PICK

1 a) How many bottles were picked up?

b) The children picked up 8 empty crisp packets and 17 cans. Where would the bars be drawn for these types of litter?

Share

a)

I drew a line across from the top of the bar that represents bottles. It is half-way between 14 and 16.

The Great Big Litter Pick

Half-way between 14 and 16 is 15.

15 bottles were picked up.

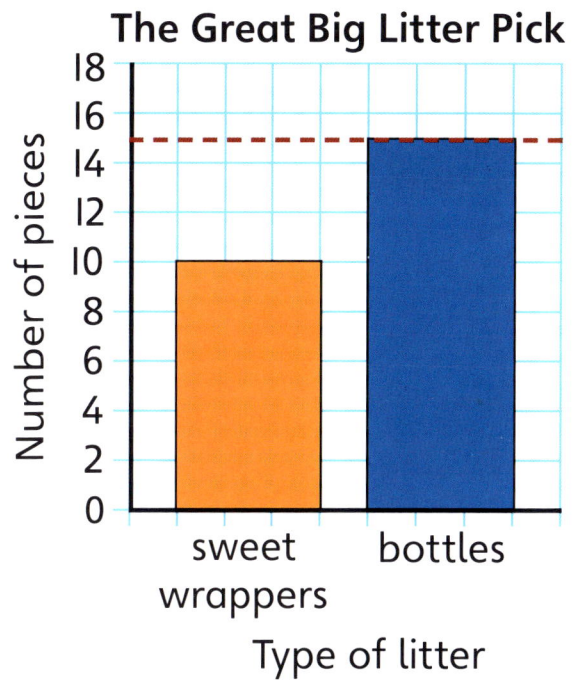

b)

The Great Big Litter Pick

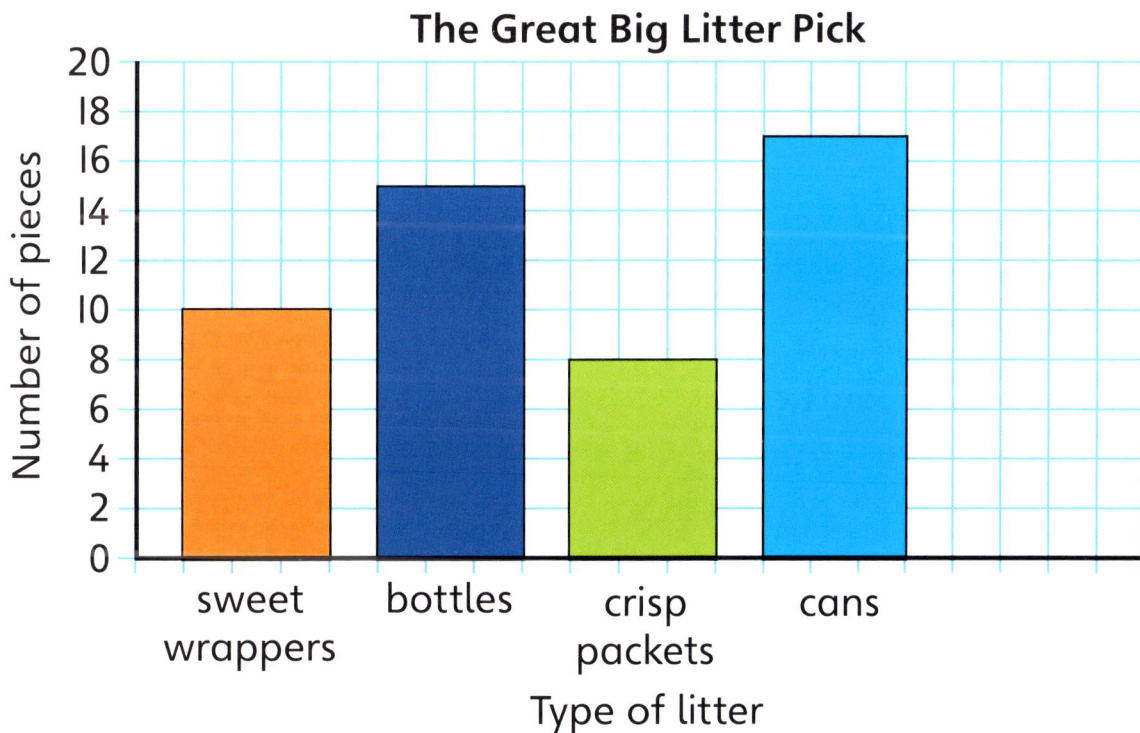

I made sure I left space between the bars. I left the same amount of space between each bar.

Think together

1 Complete the bar chart for the litter that the children collected in total.

Type of litter	Sweet wrappers	Bottles	Crisp Packets	Cans
Number of pieces	70	75	50	98

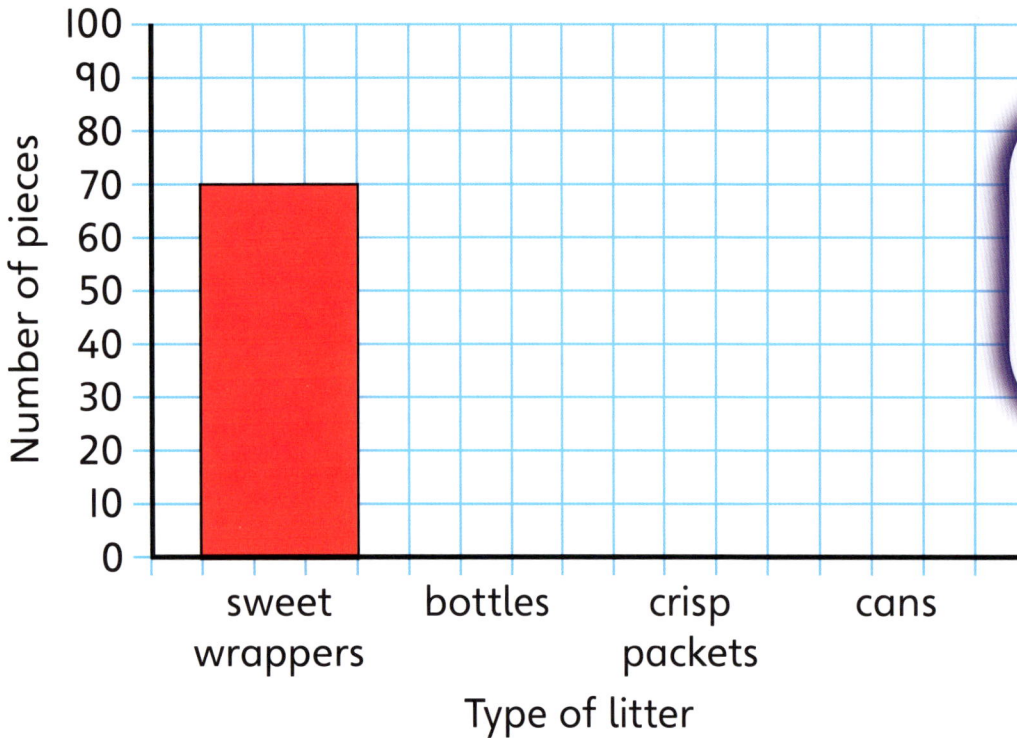

I wonder where I can put 98. It is over half-way between 90 and 100.

2 Discuss with a partner what mistakes you can see on this bar chart.

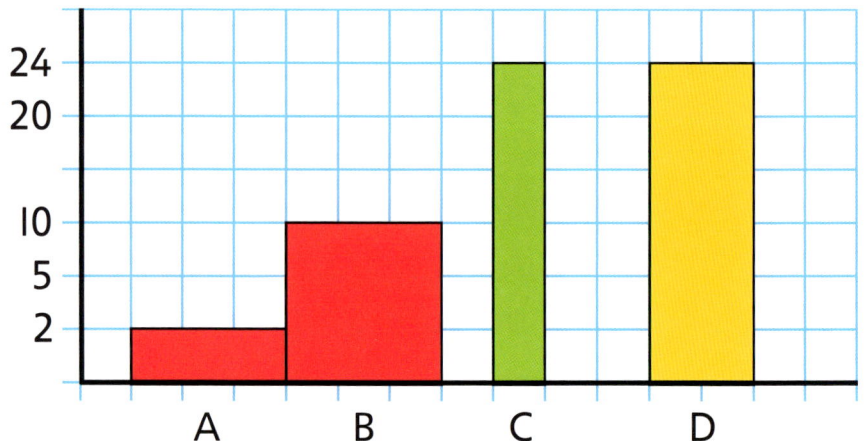

CHALLENGE

3 Think about all you have learnt so far in this unit.

Collect some data about the children in your class.

- What are their favourite hobbies?

- How many pets do they each have?

- How do they travel to school?

- What is their favourite animal?

Then represent your data in different ways.

I will use a tally chart to collect my data and then I will work out the totals.

I will represent my data on a pictogram and a bar chart.

→ Practice book 3C p133

Simple two-way tables

Discover

Field events		
	Ball throw	**Discus throw**
Ambika	14 m	21 m
Ebo	23 m	18 m
Richard	21 m	16 m
Alex	17 m	29 m

1 a) Who came in 1st, 2nd, 3rd and 4th place for the ball throw?

b) How much further did Alex throw the discus compared to Ambika?

Share

a) Look at the column for the ball throw.

Field events		
	Ball throw	**Discus throw**
Ambika	14 m	21 m
Ebo	23 m	18 m
Richard	21 m	16 m
Alex	17 m	29 m

Rows in a table go across the page. Columns in a table go down the page.

Look along each row to find out who threw each distance.

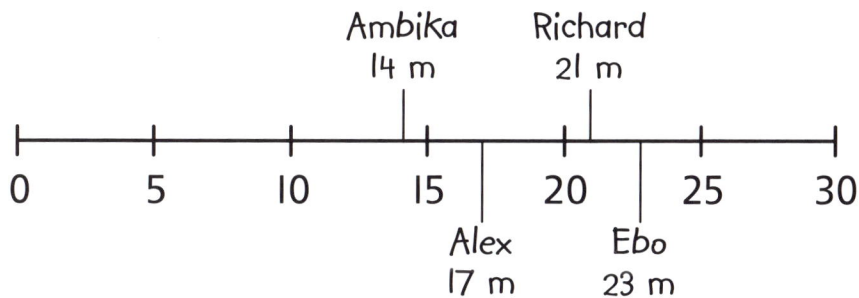

Ambika 14 m   Richard 21 m

0   5   10   15   20   25   30

Alex 17 m   Ebo 23 m

I put the numbers on a number line.

$14 < 17 < 21 < 23$

Ebo came in 1st place, Richard came in 2nd place, Alex came in 3rd place and Ambika came in 4th place for the ball throw.

b) Look at the distances for Ambika and Alex in the discus throw column.

Ambika threw the discus 21 m.

Alex threw the discus 29 m.

	Discus throw
Ambika	21 m
Alex	29 m

$29 \text{ m} - 21 \text{ m} = 8 \text{ m}$

Alex threw the discus 8 m further than Ambika.

Think together

1 These are the results from the running events.

Running event times		
	100 m race	**200 m race**
Ambika	22 seconds	49 seconds
Ebo	31 seconds	50 seconds
Richard	27 seconds	51 seconds
Alex	26 seconds	53 seconds

a) How long did Alex take to run the 100 m race?

b) How long did Ebo take to run the 200 m race?

c) Who ran the 200 m race the fastest?

d) Who came 1st, 2nd, 3rd and 4th in the 100 m race?

e) How much faster did Ambika run the 200 m race compared to Richard?

I think the fastest time will be the lowest number and the slowest time will be the highest number.

2 This table shows how many points each house won on sports day. Complete the table.

House	Running	Field	Total
Ash House	30	50	
Oak House	45		80
Maple House	40		85

3 This table shows the number of medals won by each year group.

CHALLENGE

Year	1st, 2nd or 3rd	Commended	Total
Year 3	21	15	
Year 4		9	42
Year 5	20		37
Year 6		26	48

a) Use the information to complete the table.

b) Write three sentences about the information in the table.

I think I can work out this question based on the information I know.

→ Practice book 3C p136

End of unit check

	The way Year 3 came to school
car	🚹🚹🚹🚹🚹
scooter	🚹🚹🚹🚹
walk	🚹🚹🚹🚹🚹
bike	🚹🚹🚹

Key: Each 🚹 represents 2 people.

1 How many children came to school by scooter?

A $3\frac{1}{2}$ C 7

B 3   D 4

2 Based on the pictogram, which statement is true?

A The same number of children walked to school as came by car.

B Walking is the most popular way for children to come to school.

C 3 children came to school by bike.

D 2 more children walked to school than came to school by scooter.

3 This table shows the scores of three children in their English and Maths tests.

	Maths	English
Jamie	30	25
Mo	15	32
Danny	28	20

How many more marks did Mo get than Jamie in English?

A 7 marks   B 15 marks   C 12 marks   D 17 marks

4 Lee asked some children in Year 3 how many pets they had.

He put his results in a bar chart.

How many children have 3 pets?

Pets owned by children in Year 3

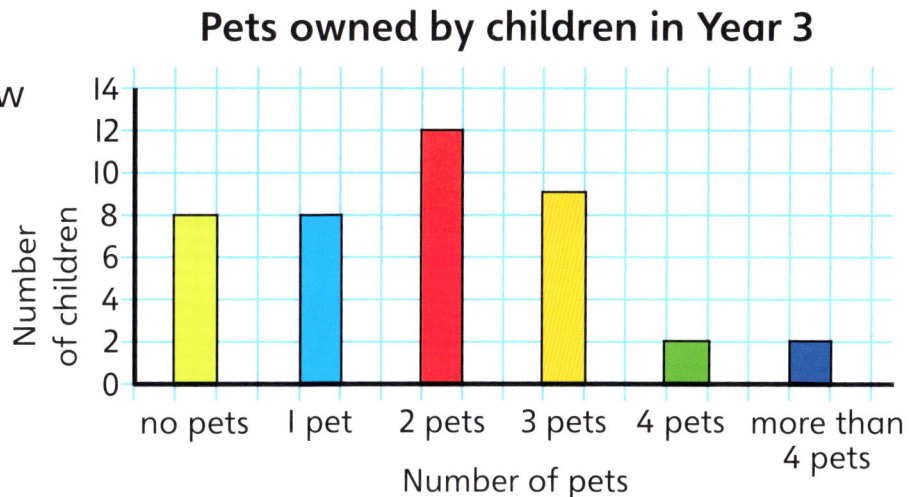

A   9   B $4\frac{1}{2}$ C   12   D   2

5 How many children did Lee ask in total?

A   37   B   12   C   41   D   20

6 This table shows the highest and lowest temperatures in Norwich on four days in September.

	Highest temperature °C	Lowest temperature °C
Friday	13	8
Saturday	16	10
Sunday	18	9
Monday	15	8

a) Which day had the highest temperature?

b) Which day had the greatest difference between the highest and lowest temperature?

c) What is the difference between the highest temperature on Friday and the highest temperature on Sunday?

189

→ Practice book 3C p139

It is always good to learn new things!

What do we know now?

Can you do all these things?

- ⚡ Add and subtract fractions
- ⚡ Convert, add and subtract money
- ⚡ Tell the time using hours and minutes
- ⚡ Recognise, draw and describe 2D and 3D shapes
- ⚡ Draw and interpret tables and bar charts

Some of it was difficult, but we did not give up!

Now you are ready for the next books!

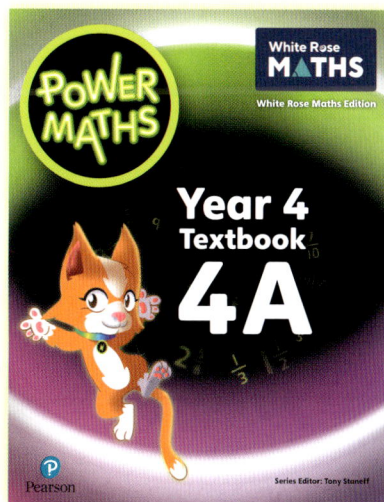

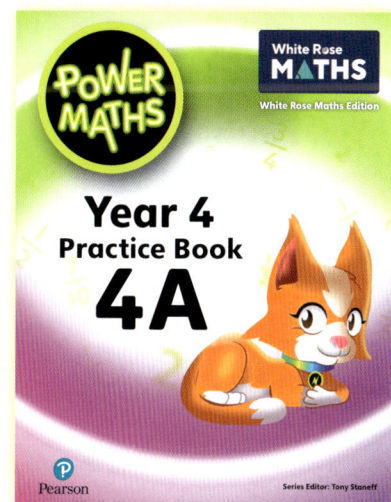

POWER MATHS

White Rose MATHS
White Rose Maths Edition

Year 4
Textbook
4A

Pearson

Series Editor: Tony Staneff

POWER MATHS

White Rose MATHS
White Rose Maths Edition

Year 4
Practice Book
4A

Pearson

Series Editor: Tony Staneff

Published by Pearson Education Limited, 80 Strand, London, WC2R 0RL.

www.pearsonschools.co.uk

Text © Pearson Education Limited 2018, 2023
Edited by Pearson and Florence Production Ltd
First edition edited by Pearson, Little Grey Cells Publishing Services and Haremi Ltd
Designed and typeset by Pearson and PDQ Digital Media Solutions Ltd
First edition designed and typeset by Kamae Design
Original illustrations © Pearson Education Limited 2017, 2023
Illustrated by Laura Arias, Fran and David Brylewski, Diego Diaz, Virginia Fontanabona, Adam Linley, Paul Moran
and Nadene Naude at Beehive Illustration; Emily Skinner at Graham-Cameron Illustration; and Kamae Design
Images: The Royal Mint, 1971, 1982, 1990, 1992, 1998, 2017, 2023: 27, 31, 42, 44–50, 52–54, 56–58, 60, 62–65, 69;
Bank of England: 42, 44–47, 49, 51, 53, 55, 57–63, 65
Cover design by Pearson Education Ltd
Front and back cover illustrations by Diego Diaz and Nadene Naude at Beehive Illustration

Series editor: Tony Staneff
Lead author: Josh Lury
Consultants (first edition): Professor Liu Jian and Professor Zhang Dan

The rights of Tony Staneff and Josh Lury to be identified as authors of this work have been asserted by them in
accordance with the Copyright, Designs and Patents Act 1988.

First published 2018
This edition first published 2023

27 26 25 24 23
10 9 8 7 6 5 4 3 2 1

British Library Cataloguing in Publication Data
A catalogue record for this book is available from the British Library

ISBN 978 1 292 41953 4

Printed in the UK by Bell & Bain Ltd, Glasgow

For Power Maths resources go to
www.activelearnprimary.co.uk

Note from the publisher
Pearson has robust editorial processes, including answer and fact checks, to ensure the accuracy of the content in this
publication, and every effort is made to ensure this publication is free of errors. We are, however, only human, and
occasionally errors do occur. Pearson is not liable for any misunderstandings that arise as a result of errors in this
publication, but it is our priority to ensure that the content is accurate. If you spot an error, please do contact us at
resourcescorrections@pearson.com so we can make sure it is corrected.